Know Your Worth

Conquering Your Past
for a Powerful Future

JESSICA VAUGHN

Limits of Liability and Disclaimer of Warranty
The author and publisher shall not be liable for your misuse of this material. This book is strictly for informational and educational purposes.

Warning—Disclaimer
The purpose of this book is to educate and entertain. The author and/or publisher do not guarantee that anyone following these techniques, suggestions, tips, ideas, or strategies will become successful. The author and/or publisher shall have neither liability nor responsibility to anyone with respect to any loss or damage caused, or alleged to be caused, directly or indirectly by the information contained in this book.

Photography: Sarah Bokone
Hair: Tori Wiltrout
Makeup: Brittany Turner

ISBN-13: 978-1-5170-6160-9
ISBN-10: 1517061601

To Jon, who is my rock and my supporter.
You challenge me every day to become a better version of myself.
To the moon and back, I love you.

To my cousin April, who led me to the Lord and
who never stopped believing in me.

To anyone who has been a part of my life:
I want to thank you from the bottom of my heart for pushing me to new
limits and always encouraging me every day to be more like Jesus.
I wouldn't be where I am today without you.
You know who you are.

Contents

PREFACE

KIDS HAVE MANY DREAMS before they hit their teenage years—dreams of being famous and something big in this world. I mean, think about it: Did you ever doubt the fact that you weren't going to be the president of the United States? They never second-guess what they want to become. So, then, why do they, as adults, stutter, second-guess, third-guess, and never do anything they dream about doing?

As time goes on people start to adapt to their surroundings more and more. When they get to school they see how many different personalities there are. Cliques form, and then criticism comes. They go through high school trying to fit in, get good grades, and be popular. It's easy to lose yourself and your voice in the midst of the crowds. Then they enter adulthood or their early 20s having absolutely no clue who they are.

Maybe you didn't grow up with parents who supported you or maybe you did. Maybe you were abused as a kid or maybe you weren't. Maybe you had a few relationships that left you more confused about your worth or maybe you didn't. Regardless of your history I want you to know you still have a future.

I want you to start to ask yourself: Why am I turning to this world to give me my security, my confidence, and my fulfillment?

I'm taking you through my own personal journey—a journey through which my heart will be on my sleeve and Jesus will be my fingers writing to you. Everything I share with you from this point on is truth, real emotion, raw emotion, and how a small 5' 2" girl at the age of 27 overcame more than what most can comprehend. I don't want this to be just another book you read full of scriptures and what I think you want to hear. Well, I still want it to be full of scriptures, but also a book that says, "I've been there, too, and you will overcome evil things from your past." A book that says, "I've been there, too, and you are worthy of a future full of His promises." Everyone experiences pain. Pain is real, and most are afraid to share their story because they don't want anyone to judge them, think less of them, or talk about them. You just get to a point in this life where when God speaks, you act. I feel like more and more people experience pain now than they ever have. The sad part is that is where they stay: in the pain. More and more people struggle to find the light in their darkness.

I'm not sure what made you pick up this book. Maybe it is because you have a broken heart and want to learn how to heal from it. Maybe it is because you are working on growing a closer relationship with God. Could it be because you need inspiration to get out of the rut you are in? Perhaps fear has paralyzed you from going after your dreams? No matter why you picked up this book I am glad you are here. Even if you do not have a close relationship with God, have never read scripture before in your life, or don't believe there is a God I encourage you to look beyond that and know that there is a powerful message for you to hear in this book.

This book isn't for one type of person. This book isn't to bash on men or women. It's not about picking sides. It's really about self-discovery. I want it to inspire all types of people going through many different sitations. You will be able to gain something from this book no matter what your background looks like, where you come from, or what you believe in. Just know that everything I write about comes from love. I don't want you to miss the message of this book by getting caught up on scripture or my beliefs. I just want to help you understand how important it is to know your worth.

I'm ready to be your flashlight to find your way out of the dark tunnel that you may be lost in right now. I hope this gives you hope like you never have had, faith that makes you unstoppable, and a kind of love that you will never want to let go of. It's time for you to start dreaming again or to dream bigger!

Introduction
The Short-Story Version

I WAS A SEMI-AVERAGE kid in high school. Who defined what average was, anyway? I wanted to fit in. For the most part I did. This girl right here was never awesome at sports. Only ever half-good at one, really. The only part I was good at was defense. I can read the other person and where they are going, but when you give me a ball and tell me to dribble, I feel like I have two left hands and two left feet. True story. I never had money to go school shopping every new school year, so I typically just got the essentials like a new pair of shoes and maybe a new shirt. Buying new clothes every school year was always the most important thing, I felt. The thing to do was drop $300 on clothes to impress people we didn't really even like. (This, of course, is my perspective now.) We never had the money to do this, though. I had to get used to reusing my clothes multiple times. Most of them I didn't like. I remember getting on the bus one day. My outfit consisted of a white Mickey Mouse shirt, black windbreaker pants (remember those—the swooshy kind?), and these awesome shiny—yes, shiny—black shoes. I am pretty sure the only reason I remember that outfit is because I went on the bus crying that day about how bad I hated that outfit.

I never could comprehend why people say they wish they could go back to high school. That's one stage of my life I wish to not revisit. Ever, actually. I just don't care to revisit my insecure past, my slew of terrible relationships, and how rumors spread. I always found out more than I ever wanted to know about myself through those rumors.

When I was 16 I landed my first job—which had absolutely nothing to do with my current career path. I still think about the time I actually was late for the group interview, peeked in, saw it was already going on, and left. That's how my first interview went. I aborted the mission because I was too embarrassed to walk in late. Thankfully, I was given a chance to redeem myself. I received a call a few days later wondering where I was and why I didn't show up. I'm not sure how many employers do that nowadays, but I am so thankful for the second chance I was given. I worked at a fabrics and crafts store for eight years. In fact, it was the only "main" full-time job I ever had in my life. It wasn't the only job I had. I picked up some minor ones on the side just to get some extra cash flow coming in. Two other places I worked, which also had nothing to do with my current career, were a race track and a golf course (mainly summer jobs).

After high school I tried going to college—twice, in fact. I was told that I should stick it out and make sure I got a college degree because some people were worried about my future. I didn't fit the typical "finish high school, graduate college" mold. God had something different in mind for me—something better. I couldn't see myself spending so much money on student loans, only to work a job that was never in my field of study anyway (seems like that's what usually happens). Disclaimer: I know *many* people who are successful and have college degrees. I'm not hating on having one; just sharing my own story of how much I didn't like it.

I went to college right after high school for the first time. I was 18 and going for my degree in nutrition. That lasted a couple semesters. I am a hands-on person when it comes to fitness. I need to be showing, demonstrating, or talking to people. There was something about it; I just knew it wasn't my strongest link. After a slew of bad situations in my life and living with my cousin, college was no longer a priority for me. To be honest, I don't know if it ever was. I was still so young, immature, and insecure with myself, too.

Fast-forward, and now I have a house. I knew I was a different person. My business was picking up and I had a whole new awareness about being an entrepreneur. In my mind, I thought that this would be the perfect time to go back to college. I felt like I had the right mind-set to study, to get good grades, and to be focused. That drive lasted about three semesters, and then I was over it. I think I was done when I realized I was paying more than $500 for a class basically so I could play Ultimate Frisbee. That ended my college career. Sometimes it's hard to not think, "Well, did I do it right?" Then I sit back and remember everyone has a special purpose in this world, and if it doesn't involve me having a degree, then I am happy about saving some money.

Back to my full-time job: I wasn't always full-time; I couldn't be, especially while I was still in high school. I worked my way from just a regular associate, to key-holder, then eventually to being one under my boss. I was roughly 18 and a full-time manager trying to manage women who were 20+ years older than I, for the most part. I am sure you can imagine some of the obstacles. At a very young age I had to learn responsibility. I had to understand how to develop leaders, be a leader, and be trustworthy enough to handle hundreds of dollars at times. I went through applications, held interviews, and hated to do role-playing. (No, really—worst thing ever.) I met with district managers and sat in on many conference calls for my boss. I could redo a planogram likes no one's business and could color-block fabric with my eyes closed. The most important thing I can take from my first ever full-time job is that God puts us in places to prep us for what is to come. When I opened my first business as a fitness coach, I had roughly four years of management experience. I was 22. When many would say I had no right to be a manager, God begged to differ. God always begged to differ. Each time I thought I couldn't do something He was right there to show me that I could.

As time passed working in retail, I just knew and could feel in my heart that I wasn't going to be doing it forever. When I found my first home-based business, direct sales, I knew being my own boss is where I would end up. The long weekends in retail and the hours that made it impossible to do anything because you had to get up the next morning to open the store seemed endless. I started with my direct sales company, Beachbody, because my passion for helping people started to ignite within me. In my mind, it didn't matter how much money I made. The important thing to me was the difference I could make in someone else's life.

Two and a half years later I found myself making as much in one month at my retail job as I was making in one week with Beachbody. For more than two years I wrote down every week that I was going to quit my full-time job. I believed in it that much. I spoke about it nonstop. I got the craziest stares and "you won't be able to do it" comments. Sometimes when people talk to you, it's the words they don't say that can hurt the worst—when they say one thing but imply another. After much thought I decided it was time to leave my full-time job. I was so scared to leave the safety of one job to go to a place where I controlled the work. Where my paycheck wasn't based on how many hours I put in. Where I didn't have to wait a year to maybe or maybe not get a raise. Never be afraid to jump! Sometimes jumping can be the most exhilarating thing you do because you never know where God will land you.

This brings me to the present time. Where I am right now in my life. The process of discovering myself and diving further into my purpose.

Most assuredly I say to you, if you have faith as a grain of mustard seed, you will say to this mountain, "Move from here to there," and it will move; and nothing will be impossible to you.
(Matthew 17:20)

The inspiration for me to write book this was nothing short of "my mind is constantly racing with inspiration and it needs to go somewhere." So you, my friends, are the lucky ones who get to read about all my craziness, my mess-ups, my completely horrific moments, my happy days, my blessings, and more. Pretty much everything God puts on my heart to share will be in detail in the chapters to come.

Chapter 1
In the Beginning

Remember your life is not hopeless. It's what you make of it.

MEMORIES FORM THROUGH OPINIONS when we are children and young adults. We listen to our parents and think everything they say to us is the truth. We watch what they do, and we form our judgments based on their actions. Key word: actions. We hear everything they say and also everything they don't say. We only know the kind of love that our parents show us. I mean, we can barely go to the bathroom by ourselves, let alone understand the difference between right and wrong.

I heard the following story about a girl being born the same day as I was in the hospital. She looked exactly like me, and I think she actually had the same first name. My family used to joke that I was switched at birth because I never acted like the rest of my family. The only thing that got me out of that story is that I looked too much like my dad.

I am going to take you to the beginning of when I started to have memories—memories in which I can still see the whole scene played out in my head. I can remember the emotions I felt. I can remember colors, noises, and where exactly I was in the trailer. If you are a parent now (I am not), you would be surprised just how much your kids remember. Before getting into the some of my most painful childhood memories, I want to paint the whole picture of how I lived and where I lived to give you a better visual of where I am coming from.

I lived in a trailer park from the time I was in kindergarten until about third grade. Trailers were basically situated one on top of another, with no yard. Most of the time the street behind or in front had drug dealers, or parents who didn't seem to care too much what their children did or vandalized. I remember hearing police sirens every Friday because someone thought it was fun to light the trash in the big blue dumpster on fire. Hearing police sirens in the trailer park didn't make you jump; you were never surprised. If anything, you probably expected it—kind of like a noise you fell asleep to.

I lived in a trailer that, from what I can remember, never had carpet in the living room. We didn't have heat, only a kerosene heater in the kitchen. I can remember the smell it left on my clothes. I can remember my parents trying to get enough money for kerosene so we would have heat. Living in a trailer park meant that, when storms came through, you had to seek shelter elsewhere. I can remember going to a park once and hiding in one of those big pipes that drain water during a really big storm. The storms and winds would rock the trailer, and I can remember being so scared as a little girl.

Childhood Memories

My parents loved to fight. Well, maybe they didn't love it, but it's all I can remember through most of my childhood. My dad's fighting always came in the form of verbal abuse and physical abuse. There was a small hallway that led to their bedroom, where the washer and dryer were. My dad had my mom pinned up against the dryer, and was holding her, hitting her face, and yelling at her. I never understood it all. I remember my mom crying multiple times. How does one, at the age of 5, help her mom not cry and get her dad off her mom? She doesn't. How does a mom tell her daughter to not settle for someone like her daddy? She doesn't.

I couldn't really even tell you what my mom or dad did for a living. What I can remember is we had one car and mostly my dad was gone. When we needed food or had money to get food we had to walk to get it. One particular day it was snowing like crazy and bitter cold. I was young. My brother and I were bundled up and walking down a main road with my mom to the store. It was what we knew: You adapt to what you have to get where you need to go.

My memory and the details of these specific memories are powerful. They have left an impact on my heart and mind forever. They change the way I view kids now, and they change the way I view people living now. I have a heart full of understanding.

It was always hard to hear about my friends going on family vacations every summer: how much fun they had, how much they got to do, and so on. Family vacations for me were very rare. And when we did go, there was constant fighting in the car. Many times I would sit there with my hands over my ears because I just didn't want to hear it anymore. It was so loud. I can remember thinking we were going to get into an accident because my dad would be throwing his arms over at my mom. My family vacations were full of memories, but not the ones you go home and talk about.

I don't want to say only negative things, even though that is mostly what I remember. I think my parents did the best they could with what they knew and what they had. So how about a positive memory? One memory I have smiling with my dad is when he would take my brother and me to the park. He always did "underdog" with us. If you don't know what underdog is, then you missed out as a kid. Underdog is when you are on the swing and another person holds onto your swing and runs under you so you go really high. When you are 5, this is just the most fun thing ever. To this day, it is one of the only memories I have of my dad that can bring a smile to my face.

Growing up around my brother means I was usually surrounded by other boys. I've heard I was a tomboy and would beat up boys when I was in kindergarten and first grade. I actually like this story—not that I beat up people, but it shows me now, in my adulthood, that I am internally a fighter. A girl who deep down inside is fighting for what she believes in and will fight through the pain.

Wouldn't you agree that we never understand what we are going through until it is the past? We realize the importance of the situation or the importance of that season when looking back on it.

Please understand, I am not saying anything bad about trailers or trailer parks. I have nothing against them. You could live in a fantastic one—a beautiful one at that. I am here to share with you that I did not. The trailer I lived in was the backdrop of some of my most painful memories from childhood. As an analogy, if you eat a certain food and you get sick from it, more than likely you will not want to eat that food again. The smell of it could take you back to that time you were sick, and that is enough for you. On a larger scale, that is exactly how I feel about living in a trailer again. Memories I don't want to revisit. Memories that are a part of me, but that I do not focus on because they do not make me who I am today.

Everyone has their own unique journey, and what I am about to share even more with you is mine.

Chapter 2
I Have a Purpose

If you keep quiet at a time like this, deliverance and relief for the Jews will arise from some other place, but you and your relatives will die. Who knows if perhaps you were made queen for just such a time as this?
(Esther 4:14)

THIS SCRIPTURE HAS BEEN stuck in my head. I can't escape it recently, and there has to be a reason why. When I read my Bible I ask God to show me what I need to see and read. I ask Him to speak to my heart and to show me things I may not see. I could read the same Bible verse over and over, yet get a different point of view from it every time. I think it just depends on what season of my life I am in.

Over the last 27 years of my life I can say that I have been through many identity crises. Growing up, I never had a constant, aside from the boys I turned to with the hope to find someone to love me. Every day people are searching for a place to fit in. Killing themselves for rank advancements, pay increases, more stuff, and so on. We want to feel loved and treasured, and we want to feel belonging.

Your purpose in this world is far beyond anything you will ever be able to comprehend.

Will You Fill Me Up?

I started dating at a very young age. I didn't know any better, and I didn't know any different. It all started with my first boyfriend. I can remember what I felt to this day almost 14 years later. (You can do the math.) It was as if I was walking around holding out a cup asking everyone around me, "Will you fill me up?"

A constant reminder is when I would go home for the day. I would find myself in the closet most nights. Hands over the ears again. The constant yelling between my parents left me crying and hating God. I never understood why I had to go through this. God always put me around people who never experienced what I was going through. No one around me could relate to me. No one around me really even knew what was going on. How could I tell someone, "Hey, my dad hits my mom, and I have no food to eat"? You just don't do that. You don't want to feel like a crazy person, and I never wanted to, I guess, come off as not "normal." My own family didn't really know what I was going through until years later, when I was in my 20s. I thought they always knew what was going on. No one saved me, except the people whom I was dating at the time.

Little did I know just how much God had His hand on me. Many, many times I sit back and think about where I am now compared to where I was even just five years ago. Oh, how times change. Oh, how I have changed. Most of the time I sit here and wonder why this or that never happened to me. I sit here and think, "If I would have done this, then maybe I wouldn't be here." Although none of that thinking is really relevant, I just can't help but think about how God really is in love with me. All the times He saved me when I didn't deserve to be saved. All the times He showed me another way when I wanted to give up.

As you continue to read, I challenge you to look back on your life. Think about the times when you thought you were alone but something happened that changed your life around. Even the bad things that happen to us can be miracles in disguise. We have to look through the darkness and know that soon there will be light.

For Such a Time as This

I can't take my focus off of wanting to know God more. I can't stand when I feel distant from Him even though I know He has never left me. In those times, I just want to lock myself in the room until I can feel His presence around me. The more time I spend in His word, no matter how long I have, I find *me.* I realize how special and unique I am. That I am designed in a way that no one else can do anything quite like I can. For you, I want the same realization.

We all have a way that we can impact the world with our unique gifts. You are made for such a time as this. I was made for such a time as this. The more time that passes, the more chapters I add to my story. I am currently in a season of my life that I have never been in before; maybe by the time you're reading this, I will have already moved out of it and into a new one. This season of my life has never been more important. My relationship with God has grown. My love for myself has grown. My grace for other people has been my focus more than ever, and my confidence to do anything in this world has become unshakable.

The whole point of me writing this book isn't just to share my story. It is to let you know you are not alone in your struggles; you are not alone in the battles that you face every single day. Knowing your worth takes time, and that time needs to be spent growing closer to God. When you start to understand His standards for your life, business, and relationships, you will no longer want to settle for that mediocre life. When you begin the process of knowing your worth you will want to strive for something better. Your confidence will be unshakable. I'm right here with you. We can do this together.

Chapter 3
Body Image Crisis

You will never be able to love yourself if all you do is listen to what everyone else has to say about you instead of what God has to say.

MOST PEOPLE ASSUME I was into fitness most of my life. They assume this because of the way I look. I am 5' 2", weigh 110 pounds, and have a muscular build. For most of my life I have been smaller and more petite framed. People try to point out to me all the time that I don't know their struggle or what it is like. I often want to reply, "Well, you don't know what my struggle is, so how can you judge me?"

Everyone has a unique journey. The more people I meet, the more I realize this. One thing, though, common to all of us is a distorted body image when looking in the mirror. You may not have a distorted image right now because you came through it, but at some time in our life we all have thoughts of unhappiness with our body.

I know many fit and very strong people who look in the mirror yet only see a "fatter" part of their body. In my mind, I am thinking, "You are smokin' hot. What are you talking about?" Now, the very thing holds true to those who need to lose weight: The person they see standing in the mirror in front of them is someone who is always 10 times heavier than what they really are. Looking in the mirror at ourselves, it is like we have this secret vision that no one else has.

"Look. Can't you see how bad my cellulite is? It's right there."
Umm, no, sorry. Can't see it. Shall I pull out my magnifying glass?
"If only I was a little leaner. Don't you see where I need to lean out?"
Ohhhh okay, yeah. I'm sorry. I just couldn't get past the fact that your bicep is the size of my head.

Distorted

I am not talking about not having goals. That is completely different. I have fitness goals and am always striving to hit them. I am specifically talking about that person you see when you look in the mirror. It is completely different from what everyone else sees. This is what I want you to come to grips with. When is it enough to be content with where you are in your fitness journey?

Most of the time our reasoning behind wanting to change is so other people notice or like us. I've worked with many women who want to lose weight so their husband will want them again. I've seen men who just want bigger muscles and a complex so they can get "hot" chicks and attention. I'm not trying to say anything of this is wrong, *but* if you are constantly doing it to reach happiness (from other people or things) you will always be left unfulfilled. Please know this: I am not trying to put people into a category. I am not trying to say all people work out just to get attention. In my experience the underlying reason is insecurity with themselves, so they seek to get approval from others.

For a long time I felt like my identity was tied to my body image. It is kind of what people noticed me by: She has muscles, a pretty face, yada yada yada. It is still what people notice me by, in large part due to the fact that it is one of my jobs and I just love lifting heavy weights. Seeing what my body can do and lift fascinates me. I can't change how other people see me. What I can change is how I view myself and my body.

Self-Discovery

April 2014 was one of my most testing times. I hurt my back extremely bad while lifting. I couldn't walk by the end of the night and ended up going to the hospital. To be honest, I don't remember much of that first week at all because I slept and laid around for most of it. Not only did I realize who cared for me, but I also realized something else that was very important: *A lot of who I was was tied into how I looked.* When something happens like that, you don't know how severe it is. I didn't know if I was going to walk again. My mind wanted to go to the extreme and then the big one hit me: How long would I have to go without working out? I was more concerned about what I was going to look like than whether my back would even heal. Thoughts came to my mind like "What if no one likes me now?" Something deep inside of me felt like the only reason people liked me was because of how I looked and not because of who I am. Needless to say, this perspective has beyond changed me. When God says to slow down, you better listen. He had been telling me to slow down for a really long time, and I wanted to have it my way. Well, my friends, when we want it our way it tends to come with a little more pain than anticipated.

I can't even begin to tell you how depressed I felt. I had probably three people come visit me and only a few check in to see how my back was healing. I felt more lost in two weeks than I had in a while. I often cried myself to sleep because I couldn't reposition myself without excruciating pain. I couldn't climb stairs, stand too long, or sit in one position too long, either. Being very immobile for a few weeks didn't help any distortion that I may have had when I looked in the mirror. I sat back in amazement because I couldn't believe how much of my identity depended on how I looked. Would people still think I was attractive with less muscle? Would someone still want to date me? All of these questions and more were constantly flooding my brain. It doesn't help when you feel like you spoke to barely anyone in the time of your healing.

Here is what I am learning to do: love myself for exactly how God made me. If I stare at myself in the mirror too long I can see the cellulite on my legs. If I stare too long I can see all the pimples on my face. When I stare too long I let the enemy run away with my thoughts. I let the enemy, the devil, try to tell me who I am instead of allowing God to.

Distorted

I don't know what your distortion looks like, or what your emotion or feelings you try to hide or cover up by your body. Most would like to tell me they only work out to be healthy and strong. "Liar" is the first word that comes to mind sometimes. Whether people want to admit it or not, they love the attention they get—and get upset when they don't get the attention they want. Somewhere in there, there is a lack. It could be an insecurity. It could be lack of self-confidence and love. Please hear me out: I am not trying to classify everyone as messed up or having issues. I just want you to take a deep, hard look at yourself and what you see in that mirror.

Who knows how long you have had these thoughts. Maybe something started it. Maybe you were made fun of. Maybe you were overweight your whole life. Maybe you were abused. You could be holding onto years of pain without ever realizing that you are.

When I was younger, my view of myself was worse. For some odd reason I remember always calling myself "fat." I don't know if all girls go through this phase, but I sure went through it. What possessed me to say that? I have no idea, but what I do know, looking back now, is how incredibly low my self-esteem was. I would grab my skin on my body and say, "Look at all this fat." I was a skinnier kid, too.

The cycle continued for a while. I remember how annoyed my friends would get by my constant "I'm fat" phrase. Eventually, of course, I grew out of that phase, but it is a constant reminder of my past and how much I have grown since then.

Recognizing your thought pattern is half the battle. Where is it coming from? Is it of God, or is it from the enemy? The good news is that you can always change your thought pattern. I'm sharing my heart with you because I can tell you I have been there in some way, shape, or form. I have hated myself. At times I couldn't stand to look at myself. I was never diagnosed with anorexia or bulimia—*but* I believe more people struggle with mild forms of eating disorders all the time, every day. I see it in bodybuilders, competitors, those wanting to lose weight, those wanting to gain weight, and the list goes on. It is living in a constant state of fear about what their body looks like.

As I continue to work on myself, I will never give up on helping other people see who they really are in God's eyes. All these things we want to be and look like that make us feel less worthy or unattractive are rather insulting to God. We are constantly competing and comparing our bodies when He is looking down at us, wondering why we are questioning how He made us. To think about insulting God like that also puts things into perspective for me. He wants to use us right where we are—no matter what that looks like.

The Thigh Gap

This was quite the popular topic when I was growing up. I still hear women talk about this, but not as much as they used to—at least the women I am around. The thigh gap used to be a huge deal to me as well. In case you do not know what the thigh gap is, let me explain. The thigh gap is when you stand with your feet together and your thighs do not touch in the middle. It was the goal. For some, it still is the goal to make their thighs not touch when they are standing with their feet together. It seemed like that was everything people were talking about at the time, and I figured I just had to have it. It was something I could for the most part control, which was my body image. I wanted to make sure I was doing the things I felt necessary to be beautiful— doing things right so that people would like me. I never realized how into my body image I really was until today, when I'm able to reflect and look at some old pictures.

I never really considered myself to be someone who had an eating disorder. I never made myself puke and I never didn't eat. The thing is, though, I stressed a lot about what went into my mouth. I don't know how much food I ever actually enjoyed in my life without thinking it was going to make me fat. Always in the back of my head with every bite and with every meal was the thought of "This is going to make me fat."

The small portions I ate living while with my parents and being "skinny" only carried over to when I wasn't living with them, and I ate the same way. I was cautious about everything and did not really have a full understanding of nutrition. My weight fluctuated depending on whom I was dating: If they didn't really eat too well, then I didn't eat too well. If they didn't really exercise, neither did I. There was not too much drive in me when I was in my late teens and early 20s. I pretty much went with the flow of whoever I was with, thinking my life would be okay that way.

I had a scale at the time as well—the dreaded scale that I would get on every so often to see where I was in weight. When I stood in front of the mirror I was someone different. Someone who lacked confidence. Someone who stood with her legs together to see if you could see through them or not. Someone who hoped her thighs didn't touch. Someone who dreaded any time she saw the scale go up and who was determined to never go up a jeans size, either. The thoughts constantly flooded me.

I know someone out there reading this right now is feeling the same way. Even if you don't have a thigh gap thoughts are constantly flooding your mind of how you look—how you don't want to gain weight and how ugly you feel. Let me be the first to say: I understand. God wouldn't put me where I am today if it didn't have a purpose. To help you to understand you are not alone in this area. A thigh gap doesn't make you beautiful. The number on the scale doesn't make you beautiful, either. The thoughts, words, and opinions of others don't determine your worth, nor how beautiful you are. You can have victory over the scale when you decide to not let the outside world determine everything for you. As I will mention multiple times throughout this book, your worth is found in God and only God—nothing else.

My Biggest Struggle

I have seen extreme competitors and followed them throughout their journey of being lean to gaining weight—a healthy weight for their body type, I might add. I follow them mostly on Instagram (because it is the easiest way to follow). What I love about those I follow is their genuine openness about their healthy eating addiction, their obsessive working out, and their negative body image. I love seeing other people being real and sharing their stories. Body image consumes so many of us. The more people share their struggles, the more people will realize that having a six pack isn't always what it is cracked up to be. Knowing your worth is *huge* when it comes to body image.

I'm pretty transparent. I am willing to share almost anything with the hope of inspiring someone. For a period of time in my life fitness was a go-to for me. Lifting weights for almost five years now has been and is a huge passion of mine. What I didn't exactly know is that this passion was slowing turning into an addiction I didn't always enjoy. Like anything, lifting can become an addiction. It's how some people cope with life. It's how some people get attention. It's how most feel confident about themselves when in fact they are the complete opposite of confident. I would like to consider myself a pretty confident person, but I realized how I view myself and my body image isn't always the most positive. I'm not saying I am fat. I'm not saying I have no muscle and am not strong. What I am saying is I look in the mirror and think, "Why am I not stronger?" or "Why doesn't my muscle show more? Is eating this going to take my muscle away and make me fat?" It sounds crazy, right?

That said, I realized how working out became more of a chore than a fun activity for me to take care of my body. I was in a competition with everyone. Two years ago I weighed roughly 100 pounds. I didn't really know how frail I looked until I went back and looked at some pictures. I guess I have always had a fear of gaining weight.

I continued to work on my own worth and my own image because I had lost my identity in my body so bad. So when I read in the Bible about having no idols it stings my heart because, well, I am my own idol, to be honest.

Do not turn to idols, nor make for yourselves molded gods:
I am the lord your God.
(Leviticus 19:4)

I worried for so long about the size of my bicep and the number on the scale. Day in and day out these thoughts took over my life. Instead of good things consuming my mind, fitness and working out were on my mind.

In time I realized again how those thoughts had crept back in without me even realizing they had. Working out is something that started to become a chore, with me almost losing passion for it. I had to stop myself and ask myself, "Why am I working out?" I have to be willing to be honest and tell myself the truth. Is it to live a healthier, balanced life mentally and physically, *or* is it just to have a nice-looking outer appearance? Thoughts like "If I eat this or that am I going to get fat?" started coming back in. I have learned I don't have to entertain those thoughts. I don't have to agree with them. I have to question whether they are from God. Do they produce fruitful things in my life or the complete opposite?

What I want to help you understand is that you are not what your thoughts say you are. You are what God says about you. You have a million thoughts a day, and if all you hold onto are those negative ones, you will never live with peace within yourself. *Ever.*

For as many as are led by the Spirit of God, these are the sons of God.
(Romans 8:14)

We are His.

I used to hate to skip a workout out of fear. I would also double up on workouts in a day. Now, I am able to skip a few days and not feel so much pressure. Most people think I am in the gym for multiple hours a day. Right now I have been comfortable with about four hours a week—four days with roughly a one-hour workout. It changes from time to time, depending on what my goals are. I understand more than ever that I am training for life. I'm always active with walking and or doing physical activities, depending on the week and season. In the summer my girlfriends and I love to have walking dates. People don't realize that your results come with ample rest and proper nutrition. I've set goals this year to eat more fruit, to start cooking even more meals, and to meal prep. So far I am doing well, but not perfect. I have never had too many specific fitness goals, and I think it was because I also forced myself to "look good" on the outside. Now, I am going to make it a point to spend time meditating even more on His word and what He says about me. It's a time to really focus on being healthy all the way around. It feels so good to be able to release these strongholds I have had in my life. For me it's about freedom. When I have freedom, I have peace. When I have peace about me, I don't need to compare me to anyone.

For the first time I am becoming free within myself to be 100-percent me. Oh boy, is this journey continuing, though. It will never end. I will just be able to handle it and control it better. I have discovered what my triggers are. I know the things that make me get on a thought process that can quickly go downhill. I just choose to not engage with those things. When I catch myself going back to those thought patterns I have to remind myself of the truth. I refuse to live in this world where my identity becomes wrapped up in how I look or how many abs I have.

I want this exact same thing for you! I want you to know your body will never, ever define anything about you. It should never define how someone loves you. It shouldn't define how you feel on the inside. Don't be carried to and fro when you are leaner some months and not so lean other months; just stay consistent with the pattern of becoming healthier each day. Focus on how you feel on the inside and, like I said, the outside will come.

If You've Got it, Flaunt It

I'm sure you've heard the phrase "If you've got it, flaunt it." If you've got a killer bod, why not show it off in some way, shape, or form? I sometimes have people say that to me when I am trying to decide what to wear. I do work hard in the gym! I'm also intentional about what I eat. I do want to feel good about myself and have a healthy self-image—*but* for the right reasons.

I don't know when it all started with female fitness competitors (influential people) dressing in such a way that made people question whether they were a fitness athlete or something else. (I'm sure you can guess.) Over the past months on social media I've noticed how things have changed drastically. I am not putting anyone down, and I am not here to bash anyone. I am only giving my perspective and will stand by it.

Many people take pictures in their lacy underwear and post them on their social media sites. From my perspective, if I couldn't walk, in person, up to my grandpa, dad, or brother wearing something, then I probably shouldn't post it on my social media. Hey, some people may be completely comfortable wearing a lacy thong in front of their dad, but not me! Some may argue that it's different, but really it's not. You're still showing the same "goodies" you would in person except you're not moving in a photo. There is a difference among confidence, showing progress pictures, and being insecure and seeking approval/validation from others. Time and time again I see women get upset because men post the most absurd, disrespectful comments on those photos. What did they think they were going to get? I run a fitness business and a studio, so I get it that your body is also a part of your business, but I want to make sure I am attracting the right kind of people into my business.

I've posted pictures of myself in a sports bra and shorts. I still post my fitness photo shoot ones. So by no means am I am trying to be a hypocrite. The ratio of me posting them, though, has decreased tremendously. I can't control what men think of me or what they say. I can control, however, how I dress for me and my own confidence. I can dress for how I want a man to respect me.

Many will find pictures like that inspiring, and I get it. There is just nothing inspiring to me when a girl is in a thong and her butt is the first thing you see while she is holding a shaker cup. I guess this is all really such a fine line. Call me crazy, but I want to keep a lot of me private, because I want only the man I'm with to have that kind of viewing pleasure. I want him to feel special—like he is the only one. When I look at the comments on some of those photos I would say about 98 percent of them are men, out of thousands of comments.

I am always reminded by this scripture to not make my focus being all about how I look:

For God sees not as man sees, for man looks at the outward appearance,
but the Lord looks at the heart.
(1 Samuel 16:7b)

When I get a man's perspective they usually tell me, "Yeah, the photos are great"—but they would never want their woman to do that. They don't want others to see what they get to see privately. Also, I'm aware every man is different. I'm just speaking about the majority of those I talk to.

Many women and men live by the comments and feedback they get from their social media sites. It becomes their identity. I need to address men here, too. I don't want it to seem like I am putting men or women down in any way. Men are just as bad about what they show on social media. Then it eventually becomes a disorder, because then they feel the need to have a six pack 24/7 because of the attention they once had. Once they start to lose some muscle or fill in a little bit, people actually will say something about how their physique has changed. This has happened with many competitors I know. Your body becomes your identity! Usually people don't even notice it until something happens to them and they can't work out, such as an injury.

My message is about knowing your worth. It's also about respecting yourself enough. Just think about the photos you post; that's all I'm saying. Have intention with them. Save your body for the one you are with. Let him or her be the one who sees you in your lacy underwear.

One Size Does Not Fit All:
Learning to Accept Your Body if You Are in the Fitness World for Business

Your body is a temple of the Holy Spirit. God bought you with a high
price. Honor God with your body.
(1 Corinthians 6:19–20)

Accepting my body took me to a whole new level of success in the fitness industry.

What does it mean to honor God with your body and your business? With social media platforms evolving, the ability to expose yourself and get seen drastically increases. Sure, you want to be in front of your audience and your niche, but everything you post resembles and reflects on who you are and what you have to offer. So what really are you offering?

As a fitness business owner, one of my goals is to help people know that they have no competition with anyone. The only competition they have is the one that they create. Progress pictures are great to share but, like I have mentioned before, it is all about how you share those progress photos that counts.

Don't get me wrong: All of the people who post these kinds of pictures have amazing bodies and have come so far in their transformations! I fully believe that they should be proud of who they are and show off their hard work. Heck, I love inspirational photos just as much as the next person. Wearing a sports bra and shorts? Okay, sure! But lacy, see-through, barely there underwear? (You know how I feel about this.) It takes what you're advertising to a whole new level.

Many people use their bodies to sell who they *think* they are. They use their bodies to get attention. They feel like it is the only way to get it. Why do I say this? Because I have been there myself. At a very young age I wanted attention because I grew up in a home in which I didn't receive a lot of love or attention. I turned to boys to notice me. The first thing someone judges you on when they meet you normally is your looks, so this quickly became what I led with. I had *no idea* who I was or what I truly wanted, but I wanted attention and to feel accepted. I wanted to feel loved. I wanted to feel like I mattered, so the first thing I could use was something God gave me naturally: my looks.

I see so many people, especially girls and woman, who remind me of myself and who I used to be. I talk about lacy underwear pictures because I fully believe there is something in the brain that triggers differently when you see someone in a bra and panties, rather than, say, in a bathing suit.

I didn't become successful at the age of 27 because I walked around in the shortest shorts and highest heels. I am successful because I have created a culture in which respect is there for both parties. Staying true to who you are is the best thing you can do for your success. God will see and honor that. Stop trying to "sell" like everyone else.

The kind of company you want to build will be based on how you portray yourself. If you want quality customers who return, who value your opinion, and who will pay for anything you have, that starts with respecting yourself and respecting your body. Remember the saying "We teach others how to treat us"? If you think getting ahead means showing all you have to give, then don't be upset when people comment and it is always about your body or what they would do with you.

I want you to know that what you do and who you are *are* valuable! This is something I have discovered, and wish I had known when I was younger and just starting out in the fitness business. I know I cannot change the way you see yourself, but I can share a different perspective and let you know that you are loved—that you are important and you matter! Not just because of what you wear or how you look, but because you are created by a God who loves you and wants you to succeed! Do you realize how much God loves you? Maybe you are familiar with this scripture?

For God so loved the world that He gave His only begotten son, that whosoever believes in Him should not perish, but have everlasting life.
(John 3:16)

Chapter 4
Finding Me Helped Me Make Six Figures

It's not about how much you make.
It's about where your heart is through it all.

I JUST WANT TO remind you how I started with my first job. There I was:
16 years old and working in retail. I was intimidated, shy, and feeling
like an outsider. In fact, I never even showed for my first scheduled
group interview. I was a few minutes late. When I walked in and saw it
had started, I was too insecure to go in and say, "Sorry for being late."
Little did I know God was going to give me a second chance at the
same job because the manager called me back wondering why I didn't
show. You are probably wondering what this has to do with making six
figures.

The jobs we have when we are younger, or maybe the job you have
now, is actually helping you get to your dream job. You are forming
your work ethic, you are forming your management skills, and you are
forming how you run your time. In the end this will determine how
you run your very own business.

God's Plan vs. My Own

I didn't know God's plan for my life when I started that job when

I was 16. I needed a job and I needed money. I didn't think I had a purpose, because for so long I was taught I was nothing and a dropout. With nowhere to turn and nothing really else to do, I picked up fitness. It was a way to be me, I guess you could say.

Time went on. I had just turned 21 and bought a house, and I was broke. I was working 40-plus hours each week just trying to make ends meet, and I needed change. When I was presented with the business I currently run now with coaching, my only thought was "People need to know that they can have a second chance" just like I was given.

There is a misunderstanding when it comes to living a dream job life versus just an everyday, need-to-make-money job. Finding your passion and business doesn't always hit you upside the head. I don't think it is luck, either. I was working in retail management, which had nothing to do with fitness. My fitness coaching business was transformed by my retail job. Yes, I developed my "dream job"—my "business"—while I was working at my retail job. Every day I had to show up to my job, which empowered me to show up every day to my dream job.

After doing this for two years consistently and taking the steps to get where I wanted to be, I hit my first six figures at the age of 24. I never knew fitness would be my passion or a God-given talent. I had tried many small things along the way but nothing stuck. Nothing got me fired up or came as easily to me as fitness did. From the age of 24 I have known this is what God had created me to do. I knew then it was just the beginning.

Too often we spend so much time majoring in minor things. Many hours of studying and student loans for a degree we hate just because the pay is good. A degree you may have felt you needed in order to feel smart, important, and worthy. Sure, you may make six figures, but who cares when you are miserable every single day you show up for work? Don't let society tell you what to major in or what your talents should be. Listen to your heart, because God is speaking to you. He would never guide or steer you the wrong way! If you are not sure what your talents are, start asking God to show you. If you love what you do and you loved going to college, then that is also awesome. Doing these things is not bad. I want to inspire everyone to be their own person and make their own choices for their career. I don't want people to feel forced to do something because they think it's "the right thing to do" based on what everyone else is doing.

Today I encourage you to not look at your job as just a form of money. Your job, whether you are working as a janitor or a freelance editor, will help you develop skills for your dream job. God has his ways of putting opportunity out there for us, but we must be willing to take it. I encourage you to read *Quitter* by Jon Acuff, an amazing book about using your day job to work your dream job!

Continuing on with My Dreams

"Is that all you do is work?" "Why can't you just come out and have some fun?" "Is it really that big of a deal?" "I can see where your priorities are."

When the hate words come at you from other people, don't react to them. I heard them so much in the beginning of my journey. You know what? I still hear them to this day!

And while being reviled, He did not revile in return; while suffering, He uttered no threats, but kept entrusting Himself to Him who judges righteously.
(1 Peter 2:23)

The questions at the beginning of this section were common questions I heard *a lot* when I was growing my business in my early 20s. I was at a point in my life where I was sick of my full-time job in retail management—sick of the long hours and working for someone else. Yikes, I was only 21. I had a long way to go until retirement—or so I thought. I was at a point in my life when I just wanted to give up, give in, and at times run away. I didn't have a place to live or a place to call my own. I didn't have a lot of extra money and I surely wasn't able to save any money. So I worked, I hustled, and I pushed myself. When you want something that bad you work for it without even thinking twice. You put things on hold and you don't go out as much, because you know you are so close to a breakthrough. There is no off-season. There is no slow season. Why? Because when you have a passion to change the world, your job doesn't end or slow down. You are constant and steady, especially during hard times.

Here are three tips that will help get you started right away when it comes to establishing a soaring business.

First, *always treat your business like a business.* If you work at home for yourself then treat it just like you would if you worked in the corporate world. Get up in the morning and get dressed; show up! There is such a temptation to slack off when we aren't seeing results, but you need to have the mind-set of an entrepreneur. Show up every day, and schedule or block off specific "office" hours during the holidays. If you plan in advance it will all be worth it in the end.

Second, *establish your priorities,* the daily steps that are non-negotiable. Priorities are the things you should weigh everything else against. You need to align your business and goals with your priorities. Mind you, there is nothing wrong with having your business as a high priority. When the holidays arrive, you have to continue with the priorities that you established previously. You may turn some things down to stay focused. Some people just may not get it or understand, but guess what? That's okay! They don't have to. You need to live your own life, not theirs.

Lastly, *stick to your to-do list.* My to-do list saves me so much time every day in my business. It is not about being busy; it's about being productive. Write it out in advance, whether the night before or first thing in the morning. Do what needs done *that day.* Don't write a whole week's worth of to-dos down for one day of work, as this can lead to being overwhelmed and a feeling of failure.

Gosh, these seem so simple right? They are most often overlooked because you want to hit the ground running. Every day I get e-mails from people asking me to help them succeed in their own business. Another question I get is this: How do you start your own business?

Hard Work Pays Off

When I started a business, I never thought it would take as long as it did to be successful. The current motto everyone likes to preach about is "get rich quick." I don't know who coined that saying, but they have to be cuhh-razy. I have never met a long-term successful person who got rich in their first few months of business or even first year of business. Usually it takes about three to five years to see changes happening and making your money back. Of course, every business is different, especially with today's technology and social media, and businesses can boom pretty quickly. I was able to leave my job in 2014, and some people in my company have left their full-time jobs in less than two years. The thing people fall short on is giving themselves enough time to be successful. Be willing to and understand that you are probably going to have to invest back into your business as well. I didn't always understand this concept, either. When I started my first business I didn't really have any money. I mean, I was putting things on my credit card. I believed in what I was doing.

As time passed, and I grew as a person and started to read more books on business, I realized how important investing in your business is. I learned how to have patience. I realized that when people say no, you are so much closer to a yes. I am also fully aware that it takes time to be successful even though my personality begs to differ. I've learned to master goal setting. To be able to create master to-do lists and to check things off each day. Also to try to remember that every little thing I do for my business counts. So many times people forget about the small stuff because they are always focused on the end prize. That little phone call you made, made a difference in your business. The things you Googled to find more information about brought you that much closer to your goal. So, if you want to talk about success, let's also talk about all those little things you did every day to create it. I bet you would realize how successful you already are.

Becoming a Better You

The little wonders of the world have always amazed me, like how the world can shift from night to day, yet we never feel it move. I couldn't help but think about that small wonder tonight as I sat with my feet propped up in a hotel swimming area, looking out the big windows and staring into the sky at the moon. There was a half-moon and a light cloud slightly covering it. As I stared off, looking into the light glow of the moon, I heard kids' laughter all around me and water being splashed about.

I sat there staring at the moon for at least 10 minutes, just praying to God, seeking His word, and believing for answers. The next time I looked up at the moon it had shifted, and I could barely see it anymore from where I was sitting. I thought, "Where did it go?" I hadn't moved from my post by the windows. Then I remembered: As times goes on, as the seconds pass, the world is also shifting around me. It never stops. Things are always happening around me.

God is moving.

God is in the midst of her, she shall not be moved;
God shall help her, just as the break of dawn.
(Psalms 46:5)

Staring at the moon brought me to this thought: God is constantly working in our lives. We may never feel the move or the shift—we may never even see the progress we are making—but we have to remember He never leaves us. He is always bringing to my attention that when He is working it doesn't always mean that things will be happy-go-lucky. In fact, He could be forming you right now in His hands, and it may hurt just a little.

Everyone wants instant success. They want to see any sort of progress right away so it gives us motivation to keep going. (Who wouldn't? Duh!) In business and in life it would be nice to know the direction you take is right because you don't want to fail. Sometimes it seems like our prayers go unanswered—or do they? We seek the right answers because doing something we have never done before could leave us falling flat on our face. It's kind of like saying, "God, tell me exactly what you have planned for my life so you can save me from embarrassment, wanting to give up, and, well, all the stuff that comes along with going into the unknown."

Here is a prayer that I pray quite often, a prayer that has shifted my business and changed the way I view my life:

"God, instead of always praying for success and for you to work on my business, will you work on *me* today? If you work on me, Lord, then I can become a confident warrior. When I am confident in you then I can be confident in all the steps I take in my business even when I don't see my work paying off. If I am a warrior in life then I am able to fight off the enemy and not let him steal my joy on a daily basis."

It reminds me so much of the following scripture, too. You may be familiar with it.

The Armor of God

Finally, be strong in the Lord and in his mighty power. Put on the full armor of God, so that you can take your stand against the devil's schemes. For our struggle is not against flesh and blood, but against the rulers, against the authorities, against the powers of this dark world and against the spiritual forces of evil in the heavenly realms. Therefore put on the full armor of God, so that when the day of evil comes, you may be able to stand your ground, and after you have done everything, to stand. Stand firm then, with the belt of truth buckled around your waist, with the breastplate of righteousness in place, and with your feet fitted with the readiness that comes from the gospel of peace. In addition to all this, take up the shield of faith, with which you can extinguish all the flaming arrows of the evil one. Take the helmet of salvation and the sword of the Spirit, which is the word of God.
(Ephesians 6:10–18)

I literally have to start my day with thankfulness. Even before I open up my eyes I am praising God for a good day—for Him to use me and also for me to speak the right words, write the right words, and listen. I have to put on my armor of God if I want to be successful in this world. In a world in which people have more negative things to say to you than positive, and with people who would rather coach you to fail than to succeed, you *need* your armor.

Our business and business practices come out when *we* come out of our own shell. When we stop comparing our success to others. When we stop trying to always beat, out-rank, out-promote all our competitors. Then we can fully step into all God has created us to be. Our business starts with us, our morals, our values, our goals, our beliefs, and so on. This translates into the kind of business we want to run. If we have no idea who we are, what we want, or where we are going, then our business suffers. It will have no direction and will feed off of every new idea being placed on the market.

God is moving in our lives even when we don't feel Him or see the answers to our prayers. God's promises are real, and when we find our confidence in Him—when we know who we are—then we can rest in His promises for us. We will *know* that, even when we don't see our success right away, we will not grow weary and we will not worry. We must keep moving forward!

His Timing Is Perfect

Just as the earth is moving right now all around us, so is God. If you have been sitting in the same place for a little while and you have been praying, God is—yes, you guessed it—still moving. His timing is perfect, and what kind of life would we have if everything we prayed about for our business and life happened right away? We would no longer need to trust God. The relationship with Him would be more of a demand than a personal one. He doesn't need us, but he *wants* us.

My friends, I say this today to encourage you. No matter how tough things may seem right now, no matter how long you have been in this spot in your business, always remember it is only temporary. You are right where you need to be in this moment. Breathe; take some time to reflect. Maybe in this season of your life you need to learn to have patience, have faith, and work on you. Remember the promises God has for your life and remember God is always moving. When you have your doubts, because you will, remember that your purpose in this world is valuable. You are valuable.

One more thing: Don't forget that as God moves we must also move. Don't just sit back and wait. You must still work and do the small steps every day. Remember that small steps add up and make a difference. Allow God to move in your life as you move, too. God will never fail you!

He did not waver at the promise of God through unbelief, but was strengthened in faith, giving glory to God. And being fully convinced that He had promised He was also able to perform.
(Romans 4:20–21)

How My Business Changed Me

I remember being a little girl living in a small trailer in a very bad trailer park. It definitely wasn't the ideal place to grow up or dream. It definitely was not warm and inviting, and it wasn't a place where you go to your neighbors for milk and cookies. I can remember how everything seemed old and rotten. At one point it was infested with cockroaches. I can remember being in my trailer, which didn't have carpet or rugs on the floor, pretending to be an ice skater and spinning in circles. I can remember wanting to be a gymnast. And what little girl doesn't dream of being a ballerina at some point in her life?

Fast-forward to when this girl is no longer little and the world is beginning to mold her into a person. Key phrase: *The world was molding me.*

When you grow up with no consistency, no value or appreciation, you tend to take that with you throughout the years. In high school, I was like clay: I conformed to whomever I was hanging out with to "fit in." I wanted to be the popular one and the cool kid, because I was never noticed in my own home. I took this into my relationships with men and even into my very first business. I wanted to be recognized, I wanted to be on top, and I was going to be that go-getter.

I started my first business because I loved the product and just wanted to be able to help people with their own fitness goals and motivation. It was all about *my* needs and what *I* wanted to accomplish. How was *I* going to sell this or that? How was *I* going to get people on board with me?

Push. Push. Push. Buy my product. Make me want to puke.

Sound familiar?

If you are still trying to make your business all about you, then you are missing out. Focus on the people. Focus on what they want and what you have to offer them. Focus on your relationship with them and how you can improve it. When you focus on that, they will want what you have regardless of what you are "selling them," and they will want to trust you. They trust what you say because you have established the relationship. Maybe you have heard before that "people don't care what you know, until they know that you care." This is exactly how I feel when I purchase something, too. I want to know the person cares about my needs, and is not just trying to hit one of their goals and make a profit. The more honest you are with me, the more I will return and buy more. You don't have to lead with your most expensive product. Show them some of your stuff you have to offer for free and how valuable that is, too. Trust me: Things will grow from there. Of course, there are personality types that want it all right up-front, and that's great. Most of the time, that's just not the case.

Here is what I have realized: Having the business has changed me because of all the people who have inspired me. My business transformed my life and caused me to see a world bigger than myself—instead of me, me, me and making it all about *my* business. When I finally shifted the focus away from making money, God began to provide and money came. I shifted my focus to helping people and new customers came. I shifted my focus and new opportunity came. We were not created so the world can serve us; we were created to serve the world. Using our gifts and talents, we can touch those who have been untouched and give life to the homeless, needy, and so on.

It's a Choice

Today I run very successful businesses not because I sat back and pushed product on people, but because I am still that little girl who dreamed of being a ballerina. Every day I choose to have joy. Every day I want to better serve my friends, my family, and all of my clients. It is a choice that we all have to make. Peace and joy are already within us, but we have to be the ones who let them out. Your business can change you if you let it. Now, don't let it *control* you; that's a different story and a whole other topic. Have goals and dreams, of course, but remember where your focus should always be: serving people.

The moment I let myself be open to change and stopped making it all about sales is when I found myself and what I loved to do and talk about. I found my engagement on social media increasing because I was relatable and not just some plastic Barbie you can find anywhere and on any shelf. I learned I was unique and had special gifts and talents. I'm not a duplicate; no one else in this world is me. I had to step into me in order to be where I am today. This is what I want you to understand: No matter what kind of business you are in, you bring something unique to that business. It could be your communication, your energy, or your decision making. You bring such a dynamic to your company that you can't understand why some people just don't get it. Not every boss out there appreciates uniqueness. I get that. Don't let that person control who you are. He or she isn't your God. I mean "control you" as in you losing your identity. I'm not saying to go crazy on your boss. I'm saying to not let their words make you lose the big picture as to why you are here on this earth.

I encourage each of you to find the time to write down what makes you excited. What is something you can do to better serve your clients? What are your special gifts that you have to offer? When you step into who you are, your business will change. And when your business changes, you can change the world.

Your Business Is Ministry

Do you realize that your business is your ministry? I think that too many people have this perception that the only way people will see God is in the church. That is so *not* the case. This is something I quickly learned as my social media presence began to grow. Facebook wasn't there just so that I could post something about my feelings for that moment or what I was going through. My posts began to have meaning because people began to relate to them. I realized that so many other people were going through the same thing. I was helping people realize they weren't alone and how much God loves them. Every day I get to bring someone close to God. How cool is that? I would have missed that opportunity if the only place I thought I was able to minister was in church. You are your ministry. How you act and talk can resemble God. The closer I grow to Him, the more and more I want to become like Him. Therefore, I should be walking it in my life and business with Him—not just on some days but every day. Stop trying to put God into only certain categories of your life. He should be in all of them. I know some of you are thinking that you are not allowed to talk about God at work. I get it. I'm not asking you to bring your Bible and preach to everyone who needs and should read it.

The biggest tip I can ever give someone is to show *love*. God is love. He created love. You can show people just a taste of who God is by loving them. I'm not saying to dismiss boundaries in order to do so, either. You can spend time praying for them as well. Be who you are and they may ask, "How do you do it?" They will want to know your secret sauce to becoming successful. It will open up a doorway for you to invite them to know Jesus. They will probably also want to know how you can be so positive all the time. That comes with knowing Jesus. His patience, His faithfulness, His tenderness, and how He tells us not to worry—people will want in on some of that. Once again, another opportunity for them to know God in the workplace.

I built my ministry on Facebook. I didn't know where I was going when I started my first business. I don't want to say "land" or "end," because I have not landed where I am supposed to be until I am home with Jesus. My journey also will never come to an end because I am constantly changing and transforming. I've seen my life transform over the years and how my platform has grown. More importantly, I've seen how my ministry has grown. I didn't even know Jesus well when I started my business. I never had a relationship with Him. To think about where I am today in my walk with Him, let alone my business, is crazy. I can barely comprehend it. So, if you are stuck in this negative, sabotaging cycle of pity parties about your work or business, think about the changes you need to make. Think about the changes you can make. Right now you are at a point where you need a perspective change. We don't always need our circumstance to change. Sometimes it's us that needs to change.

Don't let another day slip by where you don't look at your life as your ministry. How can you inspire, encourage, lift up, and help someone today? I bet you can do this at work. God has you placed there for a reason. I know the time has been probably months or years too long, but think about those who walked in the wilderness for 40 years. *Hello!* Look for opportunity. Don't just expect it to happen and fall into your lap. I love that you are praying about it, but don't be afraid to go out there after it, too! I also think about Esther in the Bible:

For if you remain silent at this time, relief and deliverance for the Jews will arise from another place, but you and your father's family will perish. And who knows but that you have come to your royal position for such a time as this?
(Esther 4:14)

She could have died doing what she did. She loved her God and believed in Him. She had faith and didn't let her fear get in the way. Don't be quiet. Don't be one who claims Jesus only in church. Bring it into your workplace. Maybe you are someone's only hope for inspiration—only hope for meeting Jesus. We are not here to please ourselves. This isn't about us. You don't know, but maybe this is your time. You could look back on this season and see exactly why God had you there. He's prepping you for your success that is coming. We don't become successful in business by wishing and hoping things will happen. We have to believe they will and also put our own effort into them. I would not be writing to you now if I did not listen to God in 2014 when He put it on my heart that I would be writing a book. I could still, in fact, be saying, "I wish I had a book published." That wouldn't do too much for me, would it?

When it comes to business I could probably write for days. There is so much out there to discuss, talk about, and learn. This book isn't about business, though. This book is about you knowing your worth as a whole. Knowing your own worth when it comes to your goals and dreams. Knowing that it's okay to run with an idea and have it fall flat. Knowing that it's okay to invest in learning material. You should never, ever feel guilty for wanting to become a better person. *Ever.* You deserve this. You are not your past. You are not your failures. You are exactly who He says you are. I believe this is a time for you to stand up against what everyone else is doing. It's time to stand for something you believe in. To build confidence, knowing God is in your corner rooting for you and is your number-one fan. It's time to stand against the enemy who has been trying to bring you down now for the past however many years. Enough is enough. Your time is *now!*

Your business is going to boom! I believe in you! #KnowYourWorth

Chapter 5
A Heart After God

Don't ever make God a last priority.

WE HAVE SPECIFIC MOMENTS in our life where things change and shift occurs. I wasn't always someone who had a heart after God. It was more like a heart after everything else to fill up my cup. It was like I was walking around to people or things, holding out this empty cup and saying, "Can you fill me up?" Then I'd turn to the next thing and say, "Can you fill me up?" After time and time again of my cup being emptied, I knew something had to change. It started with God, then it went deep into my heart.

I get asked all the time: "How do you become closer to God?" and "How do you discern from His voice?" I might not have all the answers for you, but I can tell you my story, and maybe help you along the way and encourage you, to let you know that you are not the only one who has certain feelings and you are not the only one who is confused. Discovering your own worth and finding out what brings you joy is a process, and there is such a special peace when you really just tap into the love that He has for you. And trust me: It is something that I struggle with sometimes—sometimes daily; it just depends on the season of my life. And I have to remember that He is the one who leads me and He is the one who guides me, and when I don't spend that time with Him my days are off.

My walk with God has changed drastically and I am excited to share my journey with you!

We must <u>embrace pain</u> and burn it as fuel for our journey.

I don't know how you feel, but when I read "embrace pain" I think to myself, "That's a sick joke." Who in their right mind would want to embrace pain and thoroughly enjoy it at the same time? Yeah, I have a heart after Jesus, but I don't want to deal with pain.

Let's look at what the word *embrace* really means. According to my Google search it means:

1. To clasp or hold close with the arms, usually as an expression of affection.

2. To surround; enclose.

3. Eager acceptance.

Reading those definitions doesn't get me all excited about embracing pain. Eager acceptance? Who is eager about pain coming or accepting it?

I can recall watching my grandpa read his Bible on a specific chair in their house. To be completely honest, at that time I don't think I even knew it was even called a Bible. I just remember him reading it a lot. My mom would always talk about them going to church throughout the week when she was younger. From what I have heard my mom grew up in a very religious home, and she always said she never wanted to pressure us to go. I can recall hearing people talk about being Christian, Catholic, etc. They would talk about going to church, being non-denominational and Baptist, and so on. I swear to you, it all sounded like a different language, and I hated that I didn't know what I was. Just listening to them talk, I can remember thinking, "Well, what the heck am I?" I had a sense of not belonging and a sense of being an outcast. The only time I felt that way, though, is when the topic would come up. Growing up I don't really remember being around too many friends who had a religious background or too many who went to church. Maybe I was just completely oblivious to it because I didn't know what any of that meant.

Fast-forward. Since I didn't know Jesus most of my life, life was rather empty. Let's talk more about my journey.

I got water baptized in 2010, but what does that mean? Reborn, created, and made new—yes, I get all of that. It's not always a rainbows, sunshine, and gum drops journey following Jesus. We want what we want, when we want it. *Jesus who?* We live by the flesh. We pray for God to show up in our situations and circumstances, but then we ignore He's there because, well, He doesn't show up like we expected Him to. We are left in pain and we want to blame God. *Why did you do this to me? Why do I have to go through this?* I think you get my point. The only problem is that when most people start to feel pain in one area of their life, they shift to another to avoid it. Also, many people hold onto the pain for so long that it consumes their entire being.

I really didn't know how my life would change in 2010. I was kind of expecting a quick invasion—you know, like that day something big would happen. Wrong. It's a journey—a long journey for a heart after Jesus.

Some of my favorite pastors left the church I was attending, so then I kind of became homeless, as far as being churchless, and I started listening to a lot of podcasts and sermons on the internet. Steven Furtick and Judah Smith are two of my absolute favorite pastors; I love them. And so I listened to them religiously every Sunday, and I listened to something every day from one of them. From when I started this journey until this day, I still have a hard time discerning from His voice in certain areas of my life.

Over the past years my journey with the Lord has matured. I read my Bible in the morning. I did all the "right" things that I felt like I was supposed to do. In the beginning, though, it just felt like I was going through a routine. I talked about God—somewhat. I read my Bible—without relationship. I went to church—but I did not really pay attention to the sermons. I tithed—because I felt like I *had* to. Maybe you have felt the same way at some point in your own journey, or maybe you even feel this way now. Can I give you hope? When you continue along this journey of what you feel like is a routine, He will eventually become your heart. He will invade your heart. He will transform your thinking. He will conquer areas and struggles you could never accomplish alone. The most important thing I can say, though, is that *it all starts with* **you.**

Jesus said to him, "I am the way, the truth, and the life.
No one comes to the Father except through me."
(John 14:6)

It Was Time to Get Serious

In 2013 my relationship with the Lord really got serious. That's when my heart and mind really started to change, because I wanted this change for myself. I was carrying around *a lot* of baggage from my past. It was weighing me down and affecting me in so many areas of my life. I didn't even realize the depth of it all. That's the great thing about surrounding yourself with people who truly love you: They will call you out on your crap and do it all with love. I was being healed in 2013 in many ways. I started to crave Him more and more. Truly, something inside of me wanted to pray more than I ever have. When I pray, it does something to my spirit that I cannot even begin to type in words. I started to discover my gifts. I discovered the power of prayer. I discovered my relationship with God.

I am on this journey because I truly believe God wants me to share it with you. He wants me to let you know that no matter where you are He is always there. And for a very long time I didn't know who He was. He's changed my heart more than I can even describe to you. I felt love for people for whom I never wanted to feel love. I forgive people whom I don't want to forgive, and forgiveness is a very long process sometimes, but I pray every day that God is working on my heart. And we all have very special and unique gifts. My prayer for you is that you sit down and examine your heart. Where is your heart with God? Where are you on this journey with Him? Are you doing it because you love Him, because you want to know Him, and because you want that relationship with Him—or because you feel like it's the right thing to do? Remember: God always sees your heart, and my heart was not focused on Him. My heart was on all the other things that I was supposed to do. I was tithing, I was going to church, I became a member of the church, and my heart was never in it. I didn't understand the relationship. And my focus for you is to get to the relationship part. It took me three years to get there; I am still on that journey with Him. I realize He is my father and not just some figment of my imagination. He takes care of me; He protects me; He is for me. I want you to feel the same way that I do. I am human and, like I said earlier, I mess up and I stumble, and there are days when I don't want to pray. I want to be stubborn, be human, and be fleshly—all those things. But you know what? When I try to do it by myself, I end up more sad or depressed, or mad, or angry, or something like that.

So I want you today to sit down and journal, or talk to God, or just sit there, or read, or whatever, but examine your heart to see where you are. Because if you don't know where you are in your journey right now, how will you know what to look for or which direction to take? Recognizing your struggle is half the battle, so take a few moments today and see where your heart is with Him. Do you love Him? Are you doing things for Him because you love Him so much, or are you doing things just because you feel like you have to?

Returning to the topic of pain, we may never understand why we have to experience such seasons in our life. We may never fully have all the answers to our questions. For me, a person addicted to knowing every answer to every problem, this is quite challenging. I'm a person who wants resolution. I want to know why I have to experience this pain and I want to know for how long. My friends, the thing is we have to create our own resolution to our problems. We don't need closure from people; we put the closure on them. Closure and resolution are self-attained. We can regain control and make the choice to not let it hinder our future.

Speaking of the future, let's get into the second half of the quote "We must embrace pain and burn it as fuel for our journey." The second half gives me so much more hope: *burn it as fuel for our journey.* This lets me know that the pain I am feeling right now will be used to create my future. I may not understand it right now but God is going to use this pain for a purpose. I just have to be strong enough and have the courage to face it.

At this time in my life I could easily be filled with a lot of anger and sadness as I experience this pain. Anger will do me no good. I have come way too far in my life to hold onto any more anger. It is not in my heart anymore. Of course it exists; don't get me wrong. I still feel it, but I am learning to channel it differently. Call me crazy, but I spend so much time praying for people. It really is the only way that my heart can heal when I know Jesus is tending to it. ***At times when you don't feel good enough, "perfect" enough, or special enough to this world, Jesus can just take you up in His arms and tell you that you are.***

Chapter 6
Journaling Through it All

Some of your most deep and intimate moments with God can happen when you journal.

DON'T BE AFRAID TO pour your heart out to God. More than anything He wants a relationship with you. He wants to know how you feel, what you are thinking, and that you need Him and want Him in your life.

I am often reminded that God is constantly working through us even when we have no idea that He is. Have you ever looked back at a time in your life and thought to yourself, "How did I get through that?" That, my friends, is God. Not us. God. We try to give ourselves way too much credit when all the glory should be going to Him.

This chapter contains some of my journal entries from the past few years. I share these because what I write is real—real emotions and real feelings. I never dreamed I would be writing to all of you one day sharing my story, let alone my journal entries. I have heard before that within many people's journals is an author or book waiting to be published. Don't ever discount your story. Don't ever think that your past won't inspire millions of people.

I chose these journal entries to help give you an idea of how much I was struggling. I always pour my heart out to God when I write. It's how I express my feelings for Him. It's how I tell Him I need Him. I love to pray, but writing just does something else for my relationship with Him. One thing to note, though: When I write, I might be saying how terrible things are at the moment in a way that makes things seem positive. I know my God is bigger than my problems.

I want to make it clear that these are the exact words from my journal entries. Nothing was changed. Everything I am sharing was exactly how I felt at those moments.

November 20, 2012

Lord, I need your help. I need to know/remember things will not happen in my time. But yours. Help with knowing to give it to you and let it go especially when things are out of my control. To pray to you and say thanks to you the whole day. To help me focus on you and no one else. To live to please you even if it upsets others. Some days are easier than others. Some days walking in faith is all I do. Here is what I want. Faith all day every day to take my worry away. Trust in bigger things for my future. When I try to control my life is empty. When you are in control and I let go, life is good and peaceful.

As I was preparing to share my journal entries, I was going through a rougher time with my walk. Who would have thought that my own words would inspire me? Who would have thought that I would look back and listen to my younger self? That is a prayer for you to pray over yourself. Heck, I need to pray over myself more. Yet it is only a journal entry.

March 27, 2013

Lord, as I step into faith today with your guidance I want to be stronger with my thoughts. Lead with hope and changing people's minds. Stepping closer to you. Bless my coaches today, Lord. Take my words and multiply them to many. Lord, I ask for favor today with business showing me direction and good news. Praise you in down times and praise you in great times. Remembering your love never fails.

I want to briefly discuss how positive self-talk and writing can transform your life. I played the victim role. Been there, done that. If I can get you to remember anything from me, remember this: *Your thoughts will change your life.* Whatever you believe about yourself comes to light. Whatever you believe in your heart will show in the way you treat others and how you choose to walk around. So, let me ask you: What you are constantly telling yourself regularly? I bet that you tell yourself more negative things than you could ever imagine. Half the time we do it without thinking because it is so deeply programmed into us. Subconsciously we believe we don't deserve for anything good or great to happen to us. More than likely, that stems from the past or from the way someone treated you in a specific relationship. Good news: You have the control to change your thought process. You can reprogram your brain to believe the good things. More importantly, with God invading your heart, you will have no other choice but to want to change and be more like Him.

What I am about to share with you is pretty serious and heavy stuff. Not too many, if any, would ever know what I went through in 2014 emotionally. As you have read, men have been a weaker point for me in my life. No love from my earthly father left me in return feeling empty in my adult years. The first time I can ever remember being dumped, I was 26. I was always the dumper. My heart reveals to you the pain I went through with this particular relationship. I am sure many women out there can relate to what you are about to read.

November 11, 2013

I will not let this consume my whole life. I deserve the best. To be someone's number one, not their second best or wing man while I sit here on the sidelines hearing about him having sex with other women. It is not right and it is not fair to anyone in this particular situation. I pray for the girls he sleeps with that they know one day that they are worth so much more. This is God's body. I need to honor it the best I can in my human flesh. I know what I have to offer someone is something special. The life we could live together will be powerful whoever it is. I don't know where, when, or how it will happen but it needs to happen in God's timing. I always want answers right now. I want what I want right now. That's probably why all my past relationships failed. I push, rush, and lead with sex. Lead me, guide me, use me even if it hurts, I will make it through.

Just including that journal entry makes me feel uneasy. I can remember exactly how I felt at the start of this particular relationship. (You'll read more about it in Chapter 12.) Once again, I am sharing with you these journal entries to inspire you and to let you know I am human, am fleshly, and make mistakes. Being a journaling Jesus girl doesn't mean you know everything. This is just your secret place to be with God and no one else. Watch how your life can transform. Go back through your journals if you are feeling down, and let them be reminders of how faithful our God is. When we are in present battles, we tend to forget just how good our God is. We tend to never make it past the situation. We feel stuck, hopeless, and more.

I don't want women to think that they are an option. You are God's number one. He chose you.

For you are a holy people to the Lord your God; the Lord your God has chosen you to be a people for Himself, a special treasure above all the peoples on the face of the earth.
(Deuteronomy 7:6)

Every time I read through the following passage it revives my soul. He knows everything about you and more. You can't escape His love for you even when you don't think you deserve it. It doesn't matter what we think. We have to remember what we know to be true. Read through this scripture and meditate on every line.

O LORD, you have examined my heart and know everything about me. You know when I sit down or stand up. You know my thoughts even when I'm far away. You see me when I travel and when I rest at home. You know everything I do. You know what I am going to say even before I say it, LORD. You go before me and follow me. You place your hand of blessing on my head. Such knowledge is too wonderful for me, too great for me to understand! I can never escape from your Spirit! I can never get away from your presence! If I go up to heaven, you are there; if I go down to the grave, you are there. If I ride the wings of the morning, if I dwell by the farthest oceans, even there your hand will guide me, and your strength will support me. I could ask the darkness to hide me and the light around me to become night—but even in darkness I cannot hide from you. To you the night shines as bright as day. Darkness and light are the same to you. You made all the delicate, inner parts of my body and knit me together in my mother's womb. Thank you for making me so wonderfully complex! Your workmanship is marvelous—how well I know it. You watched me as I was being formed in utter seclusion, as I was woven together in the dark of the womb. You saw me before I was born. Every day of my life was recorded in your book. Every moment was laid out before a single day had passed. How precious are your thoughts about me, O God. They cannot be numbered! I can't even count them; they outnumber the grains of sand! And when I wake up, you are still with me! O God, if only you would destroy the wicked! Get out of my life, you murderers! They blaspheme you; your enemies misuse your name. O LORD, shouldn't I hate those who hate you? Shouldn't I despise those who oppose you? Yes, I hate them with total hatred, for your enemies are my enemies. Search me, O God, and know my heart; test me and know my anxious thoughts. Point out anything in me that offends you, and lead me along the path of everlasting life.

(Psalm 139)

Chapter 7
Getting Closer

Building relationships takes time. God will be there every step of the way.

WHEN YOU FIND YOURSELF feeling empty and alone it could mean that you are searching for other things to satisfy you. I know that you may not mean to let these things happen. Sometimes they just do and we need to refocus.

Here are a few things that happen to people who tend to stray from who they are in Christ. I know this because with some I have personally been there.

1. People often lose their identity in their relationships with other people. You kind of form to those around you and don't really notice until you have completely derailed. The enemy uses people for his purpose just like God uses people, too. Knowing the difference is key!

2. People lose themselves when it comes to their weight. They believe all the lies the enemy has locked up in their head about it—that they are fat, they are worthless, and the weight won't ever come off. Their body image becomes so transformed that it starts to affect all the other relationships around them, especially with their significant other. Many people avoid the

mirror because they don't want any extra minutes of having to look at themselves.

3. People put way too many expectations on other people. People fail them and they lose all hope. Our hope is misplaced. Our faith is misplaced. We are not supposed to set these ground rules for people to please us and then be miserable if they don't. We need to become whole in our own hearts. We can't live with expectations that people will always make us happy. Reality, folks: In case you didn't already notice, people make you angry, sad, mad, frustrated, and so on. Get my drift?

4. People will try to destroy you. They will manipulate you and try to just keep you in their own corner to be used for a punching bag when they feel like it. If we do not establish our own worth we will fall victim every time.

God doesn't care if you took a break from Him. Here is the good news: He never left you! He still chases after you and is jealous for you. So many times I hear how people have taken a break from God. He is not mad at you. He already knew what you were doing before you did it. For those of you who are searching for His heart, it's not a maze you have to complete in order to get to it. You already have it. You have everything inside of you already.

I love studying the Bible. I ask God to show me whatever He needs to show me or speak to me in my time with Him. Sometimes, I find myself doing all the talking but then I remind myself I need to be still.

Be still, and know that I am God.
(Psalms 46:10a)

If I am struggling with something specific then I look for specific places in the Bible to find truth. I use my Bible app for translations or Google them. When I listen to sermons I like to write down the scriptures they quote, so that I can go back and study each particular one and see how it speaks to me. God always knows exactly what you need to hear or read. I joined a small group, too, at a local church.

This is also for me to dive deeper into my own relationship with Him. I encourage you to start today regardless of what you are feeling. I have three different Bibles that I like to rotate from. I enjoy reading the different translations, because no matter how many times you read something, it will have a different meaning to you every time. If you feel like any of the types of people I listed above, here are some of my favorite go to scriptures that maybe you could start with:

Ecclesiastes 3:1–8—"Everything Has its Time"

Psalm 46:1–2—"God Is Our Strength"

Psalm 139—"He Knows Everything About You"

Proverbs 31—"The Virtuous Wife"

Galatians 5 and 6

You may just want to start with a simple prayer just asking God to show you what to do next. There is no right or wrong. Relationships take time. It took me almost four years to get to the point of really accepting everything in my heart. It is a journey—a journey that you decide to take. His love for you is not optional. He loves you regardless, but you have a choice whether to receive His truth and His love.

Hearing God's Voice

The questions I probably get asked the most are "How do I hear God's voice?" and "When do I know it's God's will for my life?" Like I said, I don't have all the answers for you, because—you know what?— the Holy Spirit in you is going to guide you to those answers. My biggest tip for you is to quiet yourself in front of Him. I go day-to-day and sometimes I get caught up in my day. I get so busy that I don't spend enough time with Him, and I forget how important He is and the little things that He does for me, like giving me that last thing on sale or giving me this awesome jacket that that I love for $14. For those little things I always say, "Thank you, God. That's so cool. I am so excited." And when it comes to having the will for your life, I don't have the answer for you—but God does. To tap into that, we need to quiet the noise around us and spend time with Him.

Also it takes action. It takes us going out there and figuring things out for ourselves; life is trial and error. God will supply us with wisdom and knowledge, but most of the time fear holds us back from ever going forward in our lives. I had to try a couple of different avenues—things that I might not have been as passionate about. When you hit that point in your life of "this is it," you will know it. Everybody has something inside of them that comes natural to them, something that you feel that it is almost ingrained, something you might be able to speak about all day long. That, for me, is helping people. I don't know where some of the stuff comes from—I know it's from God and it's not of me—and when I'm talking to people and hearing their stories I can feel their emotion and I can feel what they are going through, even if I personally have never been there.

Those emotions and feelings, I just know, are part of my will. To be on this earth to encourage you and inspire you, that is my purpose. I challenge you to write or to pray about or to ask God to show you what those things are that come natural to you that maybe light a fire inside of you. I know you are thinking, "I probably can't make an income of this" and "What if my will for my life is being a janitor, or something?" I don't know, but I want you to know that there is nothing, no job, anything, that is less important than the next person. So I don't care what you do, how much you make, where you're going, where you live, what car you drive, or how much money is you make. All that is completely irrelevant to what God says about you, to the will that He has for your life, specifically for you.

So in order to hear that and to know how to do it, you have to do things, you have to be out there, you have to explore, but you also have to pray about it. Ask Him to show you. Like I said, there is always going to be something inside of you that there is a passion for, but typically we don't want to express ourselves or show ourselves what we really are—what really makes us happy—because most of the time we are scared that people are not going to like us for it, or think, "I would never be able to make a career anyway, so I am just going to brush this aside." That's what happens to most people. I bet you know what you are passionate about but you choose to neglect it because you fear what people are going to think about you. Today I encourage you to quiet yourself in front of Him. Just sit there, pray, focus, and go back to the things that make you happy, to things that maybe you could talk to somebody about all day long: baseball, or maybe it's basketball, or something else like painting, drawing, or cleaning. There are so many gifts in this world. I know that I am not gifted in many areas but can do a little bit of everything, but there is just one thing that I excel at the most. I want you to journal, to write, to think about those things that make you happy—the things that really excite you. You have to pray about it and not be discouraged if you are not there yet. If it's not a full-time income, that's okay. Every day just focus on becoming a better you and growing closer to Him in a relationship, and that will take you farther than a lot of people.

Attitude

You probably are thinking, "What does this have to do with drawing me closer to the Lord or even my prayer time in the morning?" Let me tell you: It has everything to do with your prayer life and being closer to God, because He is of this world, the things that are truth, and the things that are pure, the things that are honest, and love. He is so many positive things, and He gives us so many things, yet our attitude distinguishes us from the rest. And I have seen multiple times people say that they are Christians and go to church on Sundays, yet their attitude needs adjusting. Or they read their Bible every day but five minutes later they're yelling at their friends, or their husband, or their kids in a way that is not loving. I am not saying that you aren't going to have those bad days, but when we truly read the Bible and read about His words we want to become more like Him. That is what I want you to focus on. Think about your attitude toward people: Are you forgiving? Are you loving? Do you have trust? Do you not have trust? Where is your heart in all of this? We are, of course, humans and we are flesh. We're going to have bad days and days when we feel like we might hate somebody, and that's normal. But I can tell you this: When my heart did not know Jesus, I thought, "I don't deserve this. I don't need to love these people. I don't need to forgive these people," and I carried this heavy baggage around for years. I was miserable, I wasn't happy, I didn't know what is wrong with me, and I felt I deserved it, right?

As humans we just feel like we deserve this.

We deserve to be the one who has the last word, we deserve to be right, and we feel worthy of being deserving of everything—and sometimes it's not the case. So when my heart shifted over to the Lord, I started to want to forgive. I wanted to love those people who have lied to me, who have hurt me, who have done me wrong, and who have abused me, whether physically or mentally. My heart wanted to just love them. I am not saying it's easy, but my attitude toward them changed. Behind all of that pain and behind the way they treated me, I knew that there was something going on with them that they just wouldn't quite deal with, or maybe they didn't really know it was there. But typically the way somebody treats you or says something to you is the direct reflection of their heart. So when you are being mistreated or something is happening, it is typically not about you; it's the direct reflection of their heart.

For out of the abundance of the heart his mouth speaks.
(Luke 6:45b)

I really challenge you to see where your attitude is coming from. Is it coming from the heart of Jesus? Study scripture and find things that will help you through what you are feeling. Ask God to show you what you need to work on, and open a Bible and say, "All right, what do I need to learn today? Lord, show me—let the spirit guide me into—what it is that I need today." I swear I've read some of the same scriptures over again, but according to the season of my life I think, "Oh my gosh. I read this completely different than I did ever before." So I go in though with the attitude of "I am unstoppable. Lord, please forgive me of this. How can I love this person who has done me wrong? How can I forgive? What can I do to be more like you?"

One of my prayers typically in the morning, before I open my eyes, is to ask the Lord to use me—use my mouth, use my words, use anything that He wants of me, and that is my attitude for the day. Some days it doesn't go as well as planned, but you know what? That's okay. And I am here to share with you that no matter what you are going through, no matter whether you have a good attitude or bad attitude, He is going to love you. You cannot do anything to make Him not love you. He loves you unconditionally through everything. So nothing that you've done is ever going make Him love you less. Go into the day with the positive attitude, start journaling, find your scriptures, ask the Holy Spirit to guide you, and let Him draw closer to you as you draw closer to Him.

Draw near to God and He will draw near to you.
(James 4:8a)

Think about the things you can do to change your life. It's just all about your attitude, and the things that we think about and the things that we don't think we deserve—but we do deserve them and we are worthy of them.

Discipline

I really want to discuss discipline and staying focused in a world that is completely busy and with so much chaos that we tend to not know where to go next. Staying disciplined is probably one of the biggest struggles that you can face—staying disciplined to His words, and staying disciplined to know and do what is right even though what you feel might be different. Sometimes we have to forget what we feel, and know what is right and do what is right. It's like having the attitude that we talked about and it's when you start to become closer to Holy Spirit; the gut feeling that's inside of you is really the Holy Spirit telling you what you should be doing and where you should be following. Discipline is hard. You'll feel strong and you'll be reading your Bible in the morning and you'll think, "Okay, I am filled up," and then you go to work and you might run into four negative people, or you might see on Facebook or the social media sites "this is how you should be to get this." So it's being disciplined in a world in which you feel like everything else is contradicting what you know is right and what you should be doing.

I have talked about when my heart was not filled with the Lord versus my heart being for the Lord. In certain situations or things that were coming about in my life, I started to feel conviction. There is a huge difference between conviction and condemnation. The enemy likes to bring condemnation, and the Lord would bring conviction. You have to know the difference between the two. If you stay in condemnation, which is negative, and you're feeling, "Oh, I shouldn't have done this; I should have done that," it is condemnation, and that's not God. Conviction is simply knowing of "Okay, I am doing something wrong. Something I know is wrong. I can feel inside of me that it is wrong." I'm not left feeling like I am a worthless person. He is doing it because He loves me, so let me pray for wisdom regarding what I should do, or maybe I should repent and continue to move forward. Staying in this disciplined, healthy way with the Lord is definitely hard, like I said, in a world in which as soon as you step outside the house you have to put on your armor of God, and you have to be aware of the situations and what you put yourself into. Sometimes God allows things from His wisdom to happen to protect us from something that could be even more painful. So whether it is taking that man out of your life, or that woman out of your life, or maybe not giving you that promotion at work—whatever it is—you have to believe that God has a plan for you, and you have to believe that He is always working things out for your good.

And we know that all things work together for good to those who love God, to those who are called according to His purpose.
(Romans 8:28)

So when you stay true to Him and when you stay disciplined to Him, and when your heart is continuously going after Him I can't describe the number of blessings that can come into your life. I also can't describe the amount of peace that you will feel; I can't describe you the amount of joy that you can have. It is all inside of us, but we tend to lock it up and, like I said before, not show it because we are scared about what people are going to think of us. Staying disciplined doesn't mean perfection, and I want to make sure that you know that. Being disciplined doesn't mean "Oh my God, I'm never going mess up, and if I do the Lord is not going to love me anymore." That's not the case. I am not asking you to be perfect, but I am asking you to know the difference between condemnation and conviction, and to stay disciplined. We all have an area of weakness in our lives. For some, it's food, for some it's relationships (men/women and dating), drug problems, and all kinds of different things that we tend to struggle with. To stay disciplined to Him means surrendering everything that we have to Him—and that means every single ounce of who we are. I am still on that journey of just surrendering everything to Him, because I have these little pieces in me that say, "I got this, God. You don't need to help me." The more situations I go through—that He allows with His wisdom to happen to me, to show me—I am amazed at just how much I still try to hold on to things. Maybe there is some conviction going on in your heart as I am writing to you—I don't know that; you can pray and ask the Lord to show you. Maybe there is an area of your life that you might need to give over to Him that you haven't given Him before. What is it?

Action

I've said before that sometimes the best thing that we can do is just rest in the Lord and really have that quiet time with Him to become closer, and to really understand Him, to read our Bible, and to meditate on His word. Our faith really does require action. It requires going out there and doing things that we might feel uncomfortable doing. Obeying, like we talked about, is also taking action. Taking action doesn't have to be doing things; sometimes taking action is just really expressing our faith and taking the leap to be with the Lord. Action is probably one of the hardest things to do because we typically want to pray and hope it's going to happen. And sometimes that's just not the case. Sometimes God wants to meet us halfway, and He believes in us and He wants us to believe in ourselves just as much as He believes in us. So action is huge when it comes to just stepping out there in your faith.

I am a go-getter. I love going out there and I love creating goals, and sometimes I have hard time resting because I want to go-go-go, and I want to come up with the next idea or ways to inspire you, and sometimes my action gets a little out of control. But the key words are *my action*—things that I want to do versus maybe taking action and trusting the Lord in a particular area in which I don't feel comfortable. I give it the Lord: "Lord, here are are these areas of my life that you can have, but you know what? I'm still gonna kind of control these ones, but you can have the rest."

I am sure some of you reading this right now do the same exact thing: "Lord, I trust in all these areas of my life but financially I don't really trust you, so I'm gonna work 80 hours a week and not tithe anymore, or anything like that, because I know I have to do this for myself." I was that way for a very long time. I used to work all these hours, and I always felt like I constantly had to provide for myself, when in reality I needed to just have faith and take my action into faith—instead of into my jobs and other people and other things to provide for me, even though I knew God would provide for me. I still wanted to control it. So once again, it is me taking what I want to control and saying, "God, you can have the rest. These kinds of things are a little scary for me and I don't know I wanna give you the reins for those yet, so I am going to try to do it myself." That never got me anywhere but stressed and overwhelmed, and I was completely exhausting myself—when all I had to do was take a step back and say, "God, I know you've got this. I am going to do ABCD today, and whatever I get done is what you wanted me to get done for today, and the rest of the time I'm just gonna rest." Don't feel stress about the things you don't get done.

God is a mighty God, and He will take you through the things you never thought you could go through ever. I am a testimony for a lot of things, and I am sure you have a testimony; your life is a testimony. And sometimes that little bit of action that your faith requires can just change your life completely.

But do you want to know, O foolish man, that faith without works is dead?
(James 2:20)

What does action look like to you? Maybe it is saying, "I am going to take action with being a business owner, or an entrepreneur, or starting my fitness, or running this business," or "When I go to my work I'm gonna be this person"; or taking action, as in "God, here is every area of my life and I want you to have it. I don't want these. Whatever I have the control of, God, please take them." And it is giving your life over to Him—not just little portions and "Gosh, I still struggle with these little areas of my own life, of just giving them over completely." Please hear me when I say I am not perfect. I am not coming to you from a perfect standpoint; I am coming to you from experience. I am coming to you from my heart and what I feel the Lord is leading me to tell you. Spend time with Him, and figure out what it is that you, personally, need to take action on. You might already know as I am writing to you.

And do not seek what you should eat or what you should drink, nor have an anxious mind. For all these things the nations of the world seek after, and your Father knows that you need these things. But seek the kingdom of God, and all the things shall be added to you.
(Luke 12:29–31)

Chapter 8
Are You Worthy?

If you knew the blessings that were coming, you would never second-guess yourself or live in fear and worry.

I WOULD LOVE TO think that your first response to the chapter title would be "Yes, I am worthy." I just do not know if that is the case or not. Many people may say it because it sounds like a great idea, but their hearts, minds, and soul are far from it.

I used to hear things all the time like "Just be yourself" and "Know who you are." Sounds great and all, but what is the process to getting to "knowing who I am"? I'm not an expert in this, but I can tell you that over the past few years I have experienced many situations, relationships, and trials in which discovering who I was played a huge part.

See, as humans with busy lives and schedules packed with stuff to do, we tend to just go through the motions. Our thoughts become routine and almost predictable—the same victim mentality over and over again.

"Oh great, another guy/girl who doesn't like me."
"Awesome, my parents have failed me yet again."
"Go figure, this always happens to me."
"Splendid, I got cheated on."

"Amazing, friends who always gossip about me."

I've been here before. I'll just deal with it and move on. If you have been here before, then why not take a moment to slow down and figure out why you keep ending up in the same spot over and over again?

This is what is wrong: We never take time to learn. We don't slow down long enough to know why we keep repeating the same pattern over and over again. If you hate going from pain, to pain, to pain, and heartbreak after heartbreak, then why do you keep doing it?

Good question, isn't it?

I understand some situations are out of your control. You can't predict when bad things are going to happen. What you can do is choose how you are going to react to them. We get into this "Why me?" mentality. We throw pity parties and talk about the situation we had no control over for hours. Why? What did that accomplish besides letting the enemy have all of your day? Worrying isn't going to make it better. Getting mad and staying mad isn't going to change the problem. Talking about the other person won't change them. We only have control over ourselves, and it is time that we step into that role.

I know you know you deserve the best. It's just you haven't quite believed it yet because you wouldn't allow yourself in half of the situations and relationships that you do if you believed it fully.

That was my wake-up call, too.

Before something even begins, you have to think about what it will bring. So yes, it's time to slow down to prevent yourself from future pain. Does this person have qualities I am looking for *beyond* the fact that they are hot and just nice? Should I say yes to this person who needs my help? Do I even have time for that? Where is this relationship starting from? The questions can go on and on. You have to weigh them against your own values, morals, and beliefs.

When someone tells you to just be who you are, it's just another way of saying, "Stop changing to fit into other people's molds so they like you." Pay attention to the people with whom you surround yourself, because the more aware you are the better. You will find yourself maybe being quieter around some people—when you know you are not quiet.

Why is that? Maybe you find yourself doing things you never would have done until this person came around. (Obviously I'm not talking about positive things here.)

Knowing who you are directly comes from what God says about you. This is my belief fully. It doesn't matter if other people see it or not. That's not the point or the focus. It is whether or not you see it. Do you see value in yourself and your body? Do you know all the wonderful things God says about you? If you let other people tell you who you are all the time, you will end up empty and alone.

Work on being who you are and knowing who you are on a daily basis. Then when the trials come, lose the victim mentality and figure out what may have gotten you there in the first place. Be proactive, not reactive. Stop letting things control you. You are worthy.

There comes a point in your life when you want to give up. Sometimes multiple times. When the pain becomes unbearable and the only thoughts you have are to run away and hide somewhere. Thoughts that have you second-guessing your existence and what you should be doing with your life. Thoughts that derail you from everything God says about you. Thoughts that are nothing more than a distraction that want you to give up.

These are words of encouragement—nothing more: God has never given up on us. Not for one second, minute, hour, or day has He ever thrown up His hands and said, "I'm done." With that said, your story is still being written, and right now is a chapter in which you probably want to do nothing more but burn the pages and act as though it never existed. It does, though. God knew about this before you even encountered it. Don't worry so much about burning the pages. Focus on the next pages that can be written—the pages where your blessing is coming. You put up your umbrella and walked through the storm to get to your rainbow. Don't give up now.

"I cry, I weep, and I hug my pillow wishing it was you, Jesus."

I cried a lot during this season of my life and all I wanted was Jesus.

Sometimes pain can be unbearable. The pain can come from loved ones, situations, or simply the enemy using your own insecurities against you.

It is weird how we live in an imperfect world yet the expectations of perfection are so highly demanded. People live in fear of being ourselves because we are afraid of who will like us and who will not like us. In reality, not everyone will, and that's okay. People put expectations on other people to be this perfect image to us. To never make us hurt or feel sadness. When they do, they feel destroyed and alone, and the pain sinks in. That's a big expectation to put on someone—and a very tiring job for someone to try to make you happy 24/7. They are just as imperfect as you.

When all of your hope and joy are put into one thing you can end up on an emotional roller coaster all the time. When they are up, you are up. When they are down, so are you. Here is where I am going with this: God is your fulfillment. *Period.* Where is your foundation coming from in your relationships? Pain becomes bearable when we lean in even closer to Jesus when our heart is hurting. Instead we run to other people to make us feel better. They can't really say too much to you that will change how you feel. Why? Because it has to come from your own belief in yourself.

Boy, oh boy, do I still battle, struggle, and wrestle with this. I am not going to sit here without sharing my struggle. I am pretty much an open book. I have been through many things in my life. I am sure that many of you have as well. My goal is to help people understand that they can get through these struggles and that they will come out on top each time.

When I became a Christian and gave my heart to Jesus, nothing inside of me changed quickly. I didn't feel different right away. It was more along the lines of me getting water baptized and thinking that was it. That was going to change my life. I didn't realize that I also had to be the change. I needed to repent and change my thinking, regarding many different areas of my life. This scripture reminds me all the time that I need to constantly change the way I am thinking:

And do not be conformed to this world, but be transformed by the
renewing of your mind, that you may prove what is that good and
acceptable and perfect will of God.
(Romans 12:2)

Even today, I struggle with some areas. Many people will tell you they are Catholic, Christian, and so on. They will tell you everything they do for the church and whatnot, but you can tell their heart is far from God—*like I, too, once was.*

These people draw near to Me with their mouth,
and honor Me with their lips, But their heart is far from me.
(Matthew 15:8)

A Girl After God's Own Heart

A girl after God's own heart is what I wanted to be. It is what I still set out to be today. Just because I was water baptized and am a Christian doesn't mean I get it right all the time. It doesn't mean that I don't mess up and fall short of what God wants for me. Many on the outside think, "If you are a Christian, then why do you still do this or why did you do that?" *Hello*—because we are human. We are still fleshly and, yes, mistakes still happen.

Here is what I can say: Loving Jesus has done nothing but make me want to love people *more*. Yes, the lonely, the hurting, the broken, the cheaters, the liars, the thieves, and so on. Before I was made new, I never would ever think to love someone who has hurt me. It was retaliation all the way. You make me mad; I get you back. Before I knew God, I wanted to never feel the pain of being alone, so from man to man I went. Now, I am discovering how precious I am in His eyes. My whole perspective has shifted and changed. My viewpoints and my communication have changed because of the one that I love. When I finally got into the mind-set that He is my Father it was a whole new level to my relationship with Him.

So, in my moments of struggle, my moments of weakness, my moments of doubt, my moments of insecurity, I cling to my pillow wishing it was Jesus. Just to feel His peace. Just to have Him right next to me. I know He is always with me. In those moments when I am in need, I call out to Him and not anyone else. Not my phone, not social media, not my friends—no one can fill that for you (or me). No one. Stop putting that kind of pressure on people.

Chapter 9
What Does God Look Like Without Someone?

Don't depend on someone else to build your relationship with God.
You have to be the one who wants the connection deep within your heart.

YOU KNOW THOSE PIVOTAL moments in your life when certain things just stick out to you and you can never seem to let them go? I remember an exact moment when I felt like the Lord asked me this question: "What does God look like without being with someone?" Let me explain this further.

As I started to grow my faith and become stronger in the Lord I noticed that I was always with someone. When I was with them I wanted them to also become stronger in the Lord with me. My walk with God in the beginning, I don't really believe, was not for me. Maybe it was to just please God or to say to others I was a "Christian." At the beginning of 2014, when I was in a relationship with someone who talked about God, I felt compelled to dive further into my relationship with God. *But* I felt like I only did that because I was with this particular person. Most of my relationship with God at that time was to please the other person, not for me. Toward the end of our relationship, while on a flight home from California, I heard very loud and clear: "What is God going to look like if you don't have this person with you?" I never really understood it before now, now that I am not with that person, and having spent a lot of time feeling alone and being alone. On that plane ride home, as I was reading my Bible and worshipping God through music, I couldn't help but to hear that question on repeat. It's a pretty intense question, if you ask me, because my answer back was "I don't know what it will look like."

Over the year I reevaluated my relationship with God—who and what was I doing it for. Once I realized the direction my heart had taken, I was quick to begin an even further, more intense walk with Him than ever before. Through so much pain in 2014 I learned to lean on the Lord and realized, when I was bringing myself through this pain, that it actually could have been prevented if I had listened to the Holy Spirit.

That's the thing: Way too many people are working on their relationship but never working on their relationship with God. They work on it when it becomes convenient or when things are going well. Your relationships with other people with change drastically if you continue to grow closer to God. Don't make Him a last priority or someone that you slightly lean on. Many people may say they are Christians or God lovers because it sounds good.

Loving God doesn't mean your life is perfect or trial-free; that's not what I am saying. I'm simply asking and challenging you to create your own relationship with God outside of being with someone. Whether you are married, single, divorced, or in a relationship, you should be on a constant chase after God's own heart. Not allowing the person you are with to be your God. Not allowing the person you are with to be the voice of God for you. The person you are with should complement you and have their own walk, and then you both come together with God being the head of it all.

Too many people blame God and start to lose hope because He doesn't give them what *they* want. How selfish of us. When you truly look at God as our Father and us as His children, it just makes so much sense to me. I always view it as an earthly father and how he would treat his children. Wouldn't an earthly father do anything to protect his children from doing something that he knows is not good for them? Wouldn't an earthly father challenge his children to do the right thing?

If you are a parent, do you always give your children what they want, or do you give them what you know they need?

I can't help but think this is exactly how God views us as his children. We pray and, yes, we don't always get what we want, but He gives us what we need. My opinion can change every day about something. How in the world do I know what I need long term? I can't see the whole picture, but God does. We have to remember to humble ourselves and to take responsibility for our own actions as well. I love to pray, but I know that I must also *act* instead of sitting around waiting for God to drop what I want on my lap. It takes work. Our faith requires action. The perfect verse that comes to mind is James 2:14–26:

> *What does it profit, my brethren, if someone says he has faith but does not have works? Can faith save him? If a brother or sister is naked and destitute of daily food, and one of you says to them, "Depart in peace, be warmed and filled," but you do not give them the things which are needed for the body, what does it profit? Thus also faith by itself, if it does not have works, is dead. But someone will say, "You have faith, and I have works." Show me your faith without your works, and I will show you my faith by my works. You believe that there is one God. You do well. Even the demons believe—and tremble! But do you want to know, O foolish man, that faith without works is dead? Was not Abraham our father justified by works when he offered Isaac his son on the altar? Do you see that faith was working together with his works, and by works faith was made perfect? And the Scripture was fulfilled which says, "Abraham believed God, and it was accounted to him for righteousness." And he was called the friend of God. You see then that a man is justified by works, and not by faith only. Likewise, was not Rahab the harlot also justified by works when she received the messengers and sent them out another way? For as the body without the spirit is dead, so faith without works is dead also.*

Chapter 10
Relationships

We will never know or understand why we go through what we go through until we are completely through it. Then we see God's work and hands on it all—if we choose to see them.

I CAN'T SIT HERE and say that I am a relationship expert. I don't have a degree in psychology, and I am not a therapist. Sometimes life experiences are the best testimonies. It is what I have. My pain. My happiness. My sadness. My doubts. My insecurities. My confidence. All of it. This is what I have to share with you. Although I am far from perfect, I fully believe God has allowed some of the situations in my life to happen so that I can draw closer to His heart and also so I can share them with you. Life happens way too fast. Tomorrow, I could die. I could die typing this. Yes, that's harsh. Let's face reality, though: We have absolutely no idea when our time will be. I refuse to live in this world anymore with a heart full of anger, bitterness, and resentment. Why spend time fighting, arguing, and hating? How is this going to propel you forward? Also understand, though, I am flesh; therefore these things do occur. What matters to me is how I handle them from here on out.

I'm 27. I may not have all the experiences someone would have at 40, 50, or 60, but I have enough to know how I want to live my life from here on out. Way too many people never face pain—I mean truly tackle it head-on instead of brushing it under the rug. Too many people never deal with life. They hold everything in. My goal is to inspire you so that no matter your age, you can be better. I challenge you to rise up to a new level of confidence from where you are right now. This is a decision. It's a choice.

Many times I have sat on my floor and cried, wondering when God was going to fulfill the desires of my heart. I wanted to know when it would be my turn. When am I going to be the one posting pictures on Facebook, Instagram, and Twitter about me being engaged? When am I going to get the chance to make someone smile for the rest of their life and call him my Mr. Forever? I am at the age now where almost all my friends are married, engaged, or having babies. Let's face it: In a world where only perfection is shown on social media, you can't help but want what everyone else has or is posting about. *Oh look, she looks happy. Oh look, he did an awesome proposal.*

I have to remember His timing is perfect. I have to remember that my turn is right now. No more wishing life away.

Dating Rehab

Not sure how many of you would put yourselves into some type of rehab. Not sure how many of you even look at your life and say, "I have some things I need to work on." It is so easy to look at someone and think, "What the heck is your problem? Because there's no way this is my fault." It is hard to look at ourselves in the mirror and say, "Maybe I do need to work on some things." Owning your faults, your not-so-awesome behaviors, is one of the first steps in rehab.

I'm not referring to rehab as getting admitted into some type of facility. (Maybe you need to, and there's nothing wrong with that at all. You need to do what is best for you to recover from whatever you are going through.) I mean rehab as a process of reprogramming your mind to believing truths instead of lies. Rehab to me is reaching out to people who will guide me, lead me, and coach me to become the best I can be. Rehab involves pain. Rehab involves time. Rehab, most of all, is time for healing. Let's get into what I like to call "rehab time."

For most of my life, for as long as I could remember, I had a boyfriend. I want to blame it on not really having a father figure, but I made those choices. As you have read, growing up wasn't exactly the perfect, white-picket-fence fantasy for me. Even when it came to talking to my mom, it never felt right or comfortable. Both parents can be in the picture, but when they are not emotionally there for you, then it is similar to being roommates with your parents. I did whatever I wanted—pretty much came and went when I wanted. The point is I never had structure in my life. My parents never went out of their way to tell me I was beautiful, pretty, worthy, or capable of anything in this world—all the things a little girl should hear from her parents a time or two. To be honest, I can't really remember too many times I even heard them say "I love you" to me.

When you don't really grow up with your parents emotionally being there for you, where else would a girl turn to next? Men. It would have been the next thing to show me affection other than a friendship of some kind. My first boyfriend came when I was in sixth grade, going into seventh. I was 12. I was so emotionally disconnected from my parents at that point and never understood what a normal relationship looked like. I can remember being cheated on as a young girl. My girlfriends would come to school to tell me that my boyfriend was hanging all over other girls over the weekend. Why was I even dealing with this at 12? Who knows! Of course, I never wanted to believe them, either. Little did I know but this started to develop a pattern of whom I dated and how I dealt with things. At that point in my life I didn't know who God was, nor did I know He even existed. I have a very vivid picture in my mind of a very low point in that time when I would hold a knife in my hand and make little gashes on my wrist. I was too scared to ever make myself bleed; it was just enough to leave a little bit of something. All because of a boy. A boy accusing me of something I never did. I was in the kitchen and can still remember the pain I felt that day—pain from which my heart felt like it was going to burst and that I wasn't going to survive. I can remember the tears that ran down my cheeks and the yelling that took place, as he continued to accuse me of something that was nothing but a rumor.

It's amazing the things we remember at every age of our life. The gashing continued for a little longer after that. How many people even knew I did this? Until now, probably none. If they did know, they never approached me about it.

When the pain cuts deep and you don't completely let it heal it will continue to bleed over time. You can only cover it up with so many band aids and for so long before it gushes uncontrollably. Then it is time for surgery.

Time went on. I continued to date throughout high school. I guess you could say I had typical high school relationships—the kind where you think at the time you will be with the person forever, only to look back and ask yourself, "What was I thinking?" They were not all bad, though. God brought some amazing people into my life in high school who had parents who treated me like their own. They took me in, had me over, fed me, let me shower there, and so on. Actually, I don't think I would be as strong as I am today if I didn't have those people in my path to help me along the way. I will forever be thankful for them.

What most people don't know about me, though, is that I actually dated some of what you would call "druggies" in my past. I am not going to spend too much time on them except for this brief moment right now.

I was in my early teens and had no clue what I was doing. My second real crush loved to smoke weed. I liked this guy for about three years and we were on this spiral dating game thing. I never smoked weed in my life. I never touched drugs in that way, but I sure dated and surrounded myself with people who did. There are moments when I sit back, look at my life, and think I dated just about every type of guy there is out there. I have experienced things some may never experience. Wondering why I went through all of that only leads me to where I am today. I've been questioned whether I should be giving out dating and relationship advice because I haven't been with the same guy all my life. To be honest, what kind of advice would you want to listen to, anyway: the kind in which people have actually experienced it and went through it so you can relate to them, or the type in which the person only wants to preach to you and has no clue what feeling lost feels like? I want to relate to the person who has gone through the same exact thing as I did so I can learn from their mistakes. I would never sit here and give you advice on something I never went through myself.

Dating the boys I did in high school who did drugs isn't something I am, obviously, proud of. I even went as far as buying them drugs. My friends were also drug addicts. Gosh, I am so thankful for how faithful God is. Looking back I know He was always there with me. I never even had the urge to do the drugs—never. The crazy thing is that no one really pressured me, either. They knew where I stood with them all and that I didn't want to do that. When someone came around who didn't know me and asked me to, others would stick up for me. If I can turn this into a positive, I feel like God was watching out for me. It's amazing to look back and see why I am not friends with them anymore or why I am not in that season of my life anymore. Every season of life has its trials and lessons. Just be willing to look for them.

I want you to understand through your trials, and your relationships, that God is also right there. He is watching over you. I truly believe He was with me the whole time I never knew Him. There is a purpose for your life and I want you to believe it.

Chapter 11
High School Ended—Life Started

No matter the experience, always allow yourself to learn from it.

WHEN I WAS IN my late teens and early 20s, things got more serious for me. At that point in my life I didn't have anywhere to live. I met someone while I was living with a friend's parents. This boyfriend and I ended up living together.

For six years of my life I lived with a man. Not the same one. Actually, I lived with three different guys and dated each of them for pretty much two years each. The first guy and I lived in a house that his parents let us live in. There was no mortgage, but we were responsible for all the bills for the house. It was my first time ever living with a guy. It was technically my first house (even though I never owned it). I was only 20 at the time. I was so young. I actually might have been 19. I graduated high school at 18 and moved into my friend's house for a few months before I moved in with my boyfriend.

I had no clue what I was doing. I was living with someone I had only known for a few months, but he knew my situation, cared about me, and wanted to help. So it just seemed like the right thing to do. I never thought short term then. I never second-guessed my relationships then. Whomever I was with, I was bound to make it work. I never wanted to see faults and I never wanted to admit my unhappiness at times. The only times I would confront my unhappiness were when the relationship was ending and I was breaking it off. Living with someone for the first time taught me what I didn't want to do in my next one.

I say it all the time and will continue to say it: It doesn't matter how pretty you are or what you have going for you. Pain will always come. I played wife for quite some time until his comments beat me down so much that I started to actually believe what was being said to me. You are probably wondering what his comments were. They were things like "Your butt is so big." He isn't a bad guy, but we were both immature and didn't know how to have a real relationship with each other. Moving in with someone is a big deal. This was the first guy I lived with and not the last. Worrying about who is going to keep what is stressful. Moving all of your things out after a breakup is flat-out hard. The good news, though, is we are on good terms with one another. He is a good person. He just wasn't the person for me.

Next stop: living with my cousin. I had nowhere else to go at the time. I went from being free and independent to living with six people and a dog. I was never close with my family, so moving in with my cousin was definitely a huge adjustment for me. She took me in and never second-guessed it. Fast-forward a few months. At the young age of 21 I started looking for a house. That was a bit intimidating and overwhelming to say the least. At about that same time came a relationship that triggered many emotional spots for me. This was the second guy I lived with. This time, though, he lived with me since I had just bought a house.

Let me explain.

I fell for this guy because I thought older may be better—you know, more mature. You know that saying "age is just a number"? That is definitely true. Looking back now, God showed me every reason why I shouldn't have dated him. It was a relationship that should have not continued, because drunken weekends and days were just a repeat pattern of what my mom experienced with my dad. I had seen her pain. I had seen her hurt. I had seen her abused in more ways than one. I thank God today that He had His hand on me even when I didn't know He was there to give me the strength to leave. Here is the story.

I was never a bar girl. I was never a girl in high school to go to parties on the weekends and get drunk all the time. Actually, bars are one place that make me feel insecure. When I dated this guy, going to the bar was his favorite thing to do. I would torture myself every weekend going to the bar because he wanted to. I molded. I formed. I became whomever I was dating. Maybe you know this all too well yourself? I wouldn't sit at home and enjoy myself, because I had to see what he was doing at all times. It was a big insecurity for me at the time. *Trust.* No matter how miserable I would be sitting there in the bar with my boyfriend, it didn't matter because I was able to keep my eyes on him to make sure he wasn't hurting me in another way. It sounds crazy, but I am sure someone reading this has felt the exact same way. I always saw the way he was when I was around, so to think about how he acted when I wasn't around would make my stomach sick. Think now about how long I continued to put up with it only makes my stomach sick. If you are reading this and feel like you have to be with your partner 24/7 so that you can keep a watch on them, then you probably shouldn't be together. Secondly, check in with your own heart as to why you feel the need to have that kind of control.

The weekends continued at the bar, with many drunken nights with him and me fighting. When you take a sober person and match them up with a drunk person, things typically don't end well. He was an aggressive person. He was very easy to anger; you could call him short-fused. He was also a strong person. One night above all should have been an indicator to leave. He was completely drunk, checking his phone, and as we were fighting he pushed me away very hard. Every part of my body said to walk away from him, dump him, and go on with my life. As an insecure 20-something-year-old, I didn't. I went back to him, still prying, begging, and asking for answers (more stomach pains as I write that). I would wait some nights for him to come home. Once he was home he would typically spend it in the bathroom puking at three in the morning. I had to get up at seven to be at work. He was in his early 30s; I was in my early 20s. This was so not how I pictured my life.

Every ounce of my identity was locked into whether or not he wanted to be with me. I didn't want him to be mad at me. I wanted him to like me and just make me happy—so, so, so wrong on so many levels. I am not here to bash anyone and make it seem like I was perfect. I am very aware now of my faults, of my insecurities, and the jealousy I had back then. I'm allowing you to see what I allowed myself to go through. I have made amends with these people, and they have moved on with their lives as well.

Let's continue as I entered my mid-20s. The last person I lived with was quite different from the others. He cooked. He cleaned. He took care of the yard work. He did laundry and helped out as much as he could. At that point in my life I was working from home and he was working at a little store—working for his friend and trying to figure out what he wanted to do with his life. What my boyfriends did for work never bothered me. All I ever wanted them to be was happy. I wanted them to enjoy what they did.

When living with him, I had a big season change and everything started to shift. At that point we had already been living together for a year. I enrolled myself in a business and life coaching program that changed my perspective of God and also of my business. Things were moving forward fast for me. As my relationship with the Lord grew, so did my conviction about living with this person. Things changed drastically for me in my heart. Yet I never communicated that to him. It was always easier for me to not talk about it than to stick up for what I believed in and have confrontation. Sound familiar? I just never wanted to deal with any emotion. I never wanted to face the reality of being alone, which I knew was what I needed more than anything.

We turned quickly into roommates because of my own conviction from the Lord that what I was doing wasn't right. I didn't walk around the house in short shorts anymore. I didn't shower with the door open anymore. We didn't do anything sexual anymore. I didn't want to lead him on anymore. It was the right thing for me to do at the time. The next step was breaking it off.

Reality Set In

One day he came downstairs and asked me if I wanted him to pack up his stuff. I knew it was time because I had put off the talk for so long. Who was I kidding? I didn't want to be alone again. I didn't want to live alone, either. Things were comfortable. Things seemed easy. The only problem was that I was miserable inside and killing my soul slowly—not because he was a bad guy, but because I wasn't listening to what the Lord was telling me to do. It was a very emotional breakup. As his things started to leave the house, I could feel the emptiness it created. I was alone, again.

After that breakup I made the commitment to myself that I was never going to live with another man until I was married. Obviously, what I was doing wasn't working for me. I had to try something new. That something new was God's standards. I was being reborn.

When do we get to a point where we raise the bar regarding our worth?

We give people way too much of us—more than they will ever deserve. We try to give oxygen to something that is already dead. We fall in love with potential. We fall in love with someone who may never be that person God has called them to be. We start to think we are not good enough. We become bitter and lose our happiness for other people. When we fall and break, we become afraid to love again. People and their ugly ways make us not feel beautiful. True love will come when they have to find God to get to you.

I was someone who never had issues finding a boyfriend. I pretty much fell for the person who was nice and said nice things about me. Nothing else seemed to matter when I was in my mid-20s.

The next year of my life could be entitled "Dating Hell!" It may sound harsh, but the stories you are about to read have completely changed my whole view on dating. I learned so many lessons and experienced a lot of pain—probably unnecessary pain. If I would have learned from my prior relationships I wouldn't have pursued the ones that followed. I can't take anything back, nor do I want to. I'm not here to write a book to bash the people I dated; like I have said before, they are good people—just not good for me. Are you ready to learn from my dating hell in 2014?

Chapter 12
A Year from Hell

Let your toughest seasons change you for the better. Rise above what the enemy is trying to destroy and give all the glory to God.

DARK. EMPTY. ALONE. LONELY. Broken. How do you feel when you get dumped by someone you thought the world of, yet you come to find out you were not even a thought in their world—or so it seemed?

I have been holding back writing this chapter. As I sit here and write to you, I am taken back to how I felt those four months of my life. Yes, only four months. In those four months, I learned a lot about myself. For the first time, I was dumped—a rather humbling experience, only to find out deeply broken I was. How deeply I needed Jesus to tend to my heart. How my jumping from boyfriend to boyfriend had come to a halt. There was no one this time to tend to my brokenness. Just Jesus.

Let's start with this: If you are in a relationship right now, don't *ever* let the other person try to make you someone you are not, try to tell you everything you should be (because you would be better that way), or make you think that you are stupid. Above all, don't stay in a relationship in which the other person isn't respecting you. You cannot make someone else see your worth; you have to see it for yourself. When you know what you are worth and the price God paid for you, you won't find yourself in a place where abuse is regular and a compliment becomes "You should have a bigger this" or "Maybe if you lost some weight...."

It is one thing for their words to edify your life to help make you better. It is when their words are no more than superficial bologna to help boost their egotistical lifestyle. I bet you know right now in your heart that this person might not be good for you, but you would rather stay in the pain than deal with the pain of leaving. I get it. Saying goodbye to someone isn't always the best feeling in the world. Letting someone go and possibly hurting someone can make you not want to do it. Just remember: It may hurt to let go of something, but don't let that hurt outweigh the hurt you have while trying to hold on. God has better things in mind for you.

> *"Numbing the pain for a while*
> *will make it worse when you finally feel it."*
> **—J.K. Rowling**

In the summer of 2014, I held a dear friend, who cried her heart to me, in my arms. That summer I held a friend who was broken in more ways than one. That summer I put my hands on her face and told her everything she was. Everything that God says about her and everything that she probably had not heard in a very long time. I couldn't hold onto her long enough, it seemed. I just wanted to hug her and tell her everything was going to be okay. She was crying her heart out to me because the fear was so strong that it completely took control of her whole being. All I could do was pray as she was speaking. It was dark, and she used the light on her phone to show me the bruises on her legs. Those bruises marked her. She was reminded every day of her pain and fear when she looked at them. Tears poured down her face. Her body shook. She knew she didn't deserve it, but her heart was far from believing she could find someone who would treat her like she deserved. Beaten down for years, she felt like her only option was to stay there and wait it out. The only thing that kept crossing my mind was "You are so beautiful, strong, and worthy."

I couldn't contain myself on my drive home. My heart hurt so badly for her. Why? Because that pain—I know. I know what she is feeling. The pain that you think will never end. The kind of pain where you feel stuck, like you will never get out of it. I cried out to God, not really knowing what to say or do. We all make choices and decisions that bring us to crossroads in our life. We have to want to help ourselves. I am completely aware there was nothing I could do for her besides pray for her and let her know I was there. My point is not what I could or could not do for her. My point is that you (and she, and I) are worthy and deserve the best. Truly. I want you to see *you* how God sees you—not how people view you with their own lenses. You do not need to cry yourself to sleep every night wondering or guessing. God is not a God of confusion. I am here to tell you that you are deeply loved and highly favored.

> *His compassions fail not. They are new every morning.*
> *Great is His faithfulness.*
> **(Lamentations 3:23)**

As I said previously, for most of my life I went from boyfriend to boyfriend. I am pretty sure there was always someone else there before I was completely over the boyfriend before. This sounds terrible, I know, but more people do this than I realized. Now that I am off the jumping-from-boyfriend-to-boyfriend train, I see it now more than ever. As you are reading this now I am sure you are thinking, "Yeah, I have been there, too."

When Everything Changed

I finally reached the end of the road when it came to jumping from boyfriend to boyfriend the day before Valentine's Day in 2014. I had been broken up with at about 11pm the night before. It came out of nowhere. Well, it seemed to come out of nowhere, but maybe it was a long time coming. Just that day we had been talking about our plans for the next day—how excited we were and more. I was in complete and total shock. Like most people would do, I asked him to give me another chance. I said it over and over. I really just didn't like the answer he was giving me. I'm stubborn. I didn't want to accept it. *At all.* I was hoping we could work things out and make things different. He didn't budge, nor change his answer. What hurt the most was to see how easy it was for him to say goodbye. To this day, I have never been more thankful that he *didn't* give me a second chance.

Before the breakup, I never realized how low I allowed myself to get and how much I let things happen. I am not the type who likes confrontation, so sometimes I will do anything to avoid it—including lowering my standards and self-worth. I had never realized that before. In our whole two months of pre-dating I was an option. It was almost like I wanted to win the game and be the final one standing to claim my prize. I was never the only one he was seeing, and I was well aware of that. What I didn't know right away was that he was doing sexual things with other people while trying to also do them with me. Once he got done with one, he would text the next. If I didn't hear from him until night then he was most likely on a date with someone else. I can remember the heart-wrenching feeling when I finally got to see him and there would be multiple wine glasses in the sink. I knew someone else had been there doing the exact same thing that we were doing. It wasn't a great feeling. I wish that no one ever had to experience these types of feelings, but unfortunately we do until that one day when we discover our worth and that we deserve better—which was one thing I just didn't see yet. I allowed myself to endure that pain because I knew about the girls. It was just as much my fault as his.

At that point in my life I had gone almost a whole year without having sex and being reborn in my purity. I was done giving away my body to men who never wanted to know me. I was done dealing with soul ties and all the emotions that come along with them. I bought a purity ring and had people pray over me. I thought I was strong and I thought I could handle what was about to come against me. I was wrong.

At the beginning of our dating relationship I spent half of my time forcing and trying to keep his hands off me and out of my pants. It was exhausting. Yet, I stayed. I laughed and played along with the game. It was the attention I was seeking. He was paying attention to me, so I was happy. He was an attractive guy. Everyone wanted him, so

I felt great that someone like that would want me. For two months I kept my strength and didn't let anything happen. I wanted something real—a real relationship, not something based on sex and the fact that I had a great body. A relationship founded on sex is nothing more than a quickie. Well, a quickie is what I got.

I caved and didn't fight anymore. I ended up having sex and breaking my promise with God to be with this man, who clearly didn't respect me, nor see my worth! Why? Because I didn't see it. We teach people how to treat us. I let it happen. I can't blame it all on him because I had multiple chances to walk away and be free from it. I didn't, though. I stayed. We talked a lot about God and I loved it (hypocritical much?), and it was such a huge attraction for me in the beginning and throughout our relationship. I felt the conviction every time it happened and promised myself I wouldn't do it again. Of course, it would happen again, and the same conviction would rise up. I didn't want to do it. I didn't want to have sex. I let my fleshly desire take over and win. I let my feelings of just wanting to be with someone for attention win—just for moments of satisfaction. How many of you cave and do things just for moments of satisfaction only to end up feeling empty after all is said and done? It happens to us all. When these things happen, we need to learn from them. We need to remember how we felt when it happened and what brought us to that point in the first place. See, my boyfriend wasn't the entire problem. It was I who needed fixed. I was broken inside and was walking around hoping to be filled up by him. When we put our hope and happiness into people we will, at some point in time, be let down. In this case, it left me with broken promises, a broken heart, and a broken relationship.

"Turn your wounds into wisdom."
—Oprah Winfrey

When the breakup happened I hit a low point in my life. Little did I know this was about to change my entire existence. The breakup changed my life for the better. What the enemy meant for evil God will use for His good.

As for you, you meant evil against me, but God meant it for good
in order to bring about this present result, to preserve many people alive.
(Genesis 50:20)

That's exactly what happened. It just took me a little bit to figure that out. It was time for me to enter myself in rehab—not an actual rehab facility, but an emotional rehab. I needed to change how I viewed myself. I needed to have that deep-rooted self-love and self-worth that only come from God. This person was never really committed to me in the first place. His eyes were never for me. Only for everyone else— well, any attractive girl, I should say. Two weeks after our breakup he was with a new girl in church, and five weeks later he was dating her. That opened my eyes to how the people I had dumped must have felt to see me go from one boyfriend to the next. It hurt and it hurt deep. I turned to God for everything. I listened to podcasts day in and day out. I didn't want my mind to even think about anything other than God. I needed it drilled so deep into my mind that I needed everything on replay. I went to church and praised God even when it hurt to breathe.

It is hard to face someone whom you really cared about, only to see them so quickly move on.

After the breakup we had no contact for about a week. That is when I knew change was coming. Before, I would have been calling and begging for someone back. I did no such thing. Not one call, not one text. After some time went on I couldn't be angry when I saw him, because all I wanted to do was forgive him. I didn't want to carry around anger anymore. I had carried anger for almost my whole life. I was done with it. This was my time for healing. I don't need to be that crazy ex. I don't need to be crazy at all. When it is time to end something, I want to end it well. I want the ending to be a strong statement of my character and also the power of Jesus. Never in a million years would I have been able to walk away from that relationship with everything I put myself through and let happen without Jesus in my corner rooting for me and loving me. I am reminded in 1 Corinthians 15:57 that "*I have victory through Christ.*"

Chapter 13
Don't Be That "Crazy" Girl

This one's for the girls.

I DON'T KNOW WHERE this started, but a common phrase I hear a lot is "She's crazy." Since I get to work with so many people, I also get to talk with people who have many different points of view. When someone says that so and so is crazy, I am very interested to know what makes them call that person crazy. So, when relationship talks come up I am intrigued to see how someone views the opposite sex. I take it in and analyze the opposing viewpoint. I never try to prove anyone wrong, and I never want someone to feel as though their feelings are invalid. More than anything, I want people to understand just how different men and women are—literally, how we were created by God. Not how we were formed by past relationships but how physiologically we are made up. How we are wired and programmed to think differently. Our desires and wants may look different but end up almost being the same. Men and women process things differently.

If we could understand that God created us differently and that we won't always have each other figured out, then we would be more accepting. Why? Because we won't expect the other person to fit the mold and be everything we want them to be. A woman is just not going to think like a guy. She will be able to see his perspective, but she will never ever be able to process things the way he will be able to.

Since we are all so different and typically not accepting of each other, it causes the other person to look "crazy." Don't get me wrong: I know some people go to the extreme (and I will touch on that), but we really need to stop spreading this message about women. It really boils down to maturity. We have all had bad relationships. We have all had people do things that just didn't seem right. Can I give you the inside perspective or maybe the God perspective? People do things not because they are crazy. It is much deeper than that. People do things out of insecurity and false identity in who they are. If you look at people as a whole, we all have insecurities and at times find our identity in the wrong things. The problem is, most people never look at themselves and see they, too, are flawed and imperfect. They never really own that—which makes it hard to extend grace to someone else.

I am fully aware that some people will do the most absurd things. You do not need to drive by their house multiple times after your breakup to see if they are there and with someone else. You do not need to go to their home and bang on the windows, asking if you can come in. Stop calling, stop texting, and stop threatening to kill yourself because they broke up with you. Sending someone 20 texts in a day begging them to take you back says nothing about them and everything about you. My friends, you are broken. Please, I care way too much about you for you not to see your worth. Take a moment. Take a breath. Give yourself some time. Give the person who broke up with you some time. Doing all of those things may only verify the reason why they broke up with you in the first place. The other person may not be your problem. You may be your own problem. You could be so hurt from other, past relationships that you don't even realize it because you have gone from relationship to relationship. All of that hurt has been brought into your current relationship. All the insecurities have only grown. Hurt, pain, and insecurities will make you do things you might not do if you were confident in who you were. Those things will always be there, but they will be managed and under control when you see your worth.

Can I encourage you now to, when a breakup happens, find no need to retaliate or beg for someone back? If that person wants to be with you, they will. God is not a God of confusion.

For God is not a God of confusion but of peace.
(1 Corinthians 14:33)

You do not need to blow up his phone, ladies, asking for him to give you a second chance when maybe he didn't deserve the first chance. (I know how you are, ladies, because I once did this.) Sometimes the easiest way of thinking about things is knowing you just weren't meant to be together. It sounds simple, but why force something when it should flow natural? Why are you trying to change the person you are with into someone you want them to be? If you are in constant change mode, then that person is not for you. Sure, they may love the Lord, be super-hot, and so on, but that doesn't mean there are not more people out there just like that. The only difference? That one will be meant for you. You won't have second thoughts. You won't doubt it. You will know in your heart.

Chapter 14
The Time I Was Too Short

Laugh at the times when you should have known better. Don't stay stuck there with your shoulda, coulda, wouldas.

MY DATING LIFE IS not one to be proud of. It is one, though, that I can learn, laugh, and grow from. The most interesting dating year in my life was 2014. I learned a lot of lessons about being in a relationship, and most importantly I learned a lot about myself.

Most people would look at me and view me as a person who has no struggles and the most positive attitude about life—a girl who probably gets all the dates and could get any guy she wanted. Who wouldn't want to date me? Someone who is successful, fit, and nice. Puke, vomit, throw-up talk right there. Well, folks, *a lot* of people wouldn't. If I hear one more time that I could get any guy I want, I think I'll stab a fork in my eye. (Not really.)

I meet with a lot of people on a regular basis. Most of the words that come out of their mouths are about change—wanting something about themselves to change or wanting another person to change. I guess my question is: When do we forget about always changing and embrace who we are right now? I get it. You should have goals and want to change for the better. The problem lies, though, in the need to want to change and live constantly in the future of what we want to be. When was the last time you said, "This is me. Thank you, God, for working on me and my current state." Probably not recently. I am often reminded of one of the most popular scriptures that people recite, yet they don't read the parts before it:

Not that I was ever in need, for I have learned how to be content with whatever I have. I know how to live on almost nothing or with everything. I have learned the secret of living in every situation, whether it is with a full stomach or empty, with plenty or little. For I can do everything through Christ, who gives me strength.
(Philippians 4:11-13 (NLT))

Every time I read through this scripture, the word *content* always pops out at me like a sore thumb. *Content.* Ugh. That word. Being content with where you are and who you are and what you have. That is one of the biggest struggles I face today. I am sure you face it today as well.

You are probably wondering what this has to do with dating. A lot, actually. Dating is its own world. I am not talking about making things exclusive. I am simply talking about getting to know someone and going out with them just to see if things would work. I seemed to miss this step in my younger years, but I am becoming familiar with it all too well. I was that girl who met a guy, made it exclusive within a few days, and then—what do you know?—was in love the next week. Okay, you are not the one. I'll dump you, then repeat steps 1–3 again. That's tiring and emotionally exhausting, isn't it?

We all have a desire to be wanted and to be loved. Men do, too; most of them just don't know it yet. (I kid, I kid—somewhat.) We want someone to like us just as much as we like them. Boy, oh boy, is that a hard one. Well, of course it is, because I am trying to do it on my own instead of letting God lead. That's a different story for another chapter. In this chapter, I am sharing some real-life emotions—real-life situations that have happened to me. I, too, struggle. Most people just don't want to believe it.

This next experience I'm sharing will hopefully help you make a decision—a decision about whether you are where you are supposed to be right now. I encourage you to really listen to the Holy Spirit inside of you. God is always whispering and talking to us, but He is never going to yell over our own fleshly desires. Those are our own choices. Typically what comes next is pain. God is constantly tugging at your heart, wanting to lead you in the right direction. I encourage you to slow down, pray more, and listen to your gut (which is the Holy Spirit typically sending you signals of *WARNING, WARNING*).

In 2014 I was on this crazy, wild ride of horrible dates. Do horrible dates mean I am only that much closer to getting a good date? What are the odds in this scenario? I don't know. I haven't Googled it yet to find out. All I know is I have been on my fair share.

We usually have some list in our head about what we want our significant other to look like—the qualities we want them to have and so forth. I mean, who really cares about what someone's goals are, what they want their future to look like, and stuff like that? All that is way too boring and way too serious to even talk about. As long as they are hot, are pretty, and have a bod on them, and a huge deciding factor is if you will have sex with them or not, what more could one ask for? **(Insert sarcasm voice here.)**

More and more people spend more time getting to know someone's body than they do getting to know the person's heart and soul. I hear quite often how people wish other people would change or have something different about them: longer hair, shorter hair, no hair, brown eyes, bigger butt, smaller boobs, and so on. Are you catching what I am throwing? Why are you with someone if you constantly are trying to change every single thing about them? Also, why is any superficial thing about them a deciding factor regarding how good their heart is? What I am trying to say here is: Why are you wasting your time with someone you know deep inside you are not supposed to be with? I am not saying you shouldn't be attracted to your significant other. But wishing isn't going to get you anywhere. Forcing them to try to change for you will not make them a better person. Since when are they Play-Doh? Since when are you the potter? I have been around people who tell me a list of things wrong with the person they are with.

Side note: I am aware it may not always be the things wrong with the other person; the person stating the list could be just as in need of an emotional heart check. This is more so for the people who know—who have a gut feeling—that the relationship they are in will not last. Half of the time when I ask people, "Could you see yourself marrying the person right now *as they are?*" the reply is "I don't know" or simply "I don't think so." This is when you know you are in a purposeless, meaningless relationship—a relationship with which you are filling a void of loneliness and that is causing you probably more pain than being alone anyway. You are settling for something rather than knowing you deserve better. You'll take anything. Break your morals. Let them slash your beliefs just so you don't have to be alone.

Hand raised. Been there. Done that.

A Funny Story

Recently, on one of my dates I was told that he typically doesn't date anyone under 5' 4". Have I mentioned I am only 5' 2"? Yep, I didn't make the cut. He was 6' 6", but I didn't know my height had anything to do with how I treated anyone. That time I was too short. I had been talking to this person and getting to know him for about two months. I had planned a visit to spend time with him. (He lived in another state.) Well, two weeks prior, I felt a shift inside of me and the way things were going. (This is that *WARNING, WARNING* sign I was telling you about.) I asked him twice if everything was still okay about me coming to see him. He, of course, said yes. I was talking with my friend only a few short days before I left, saying something didn't feel right and I thought he was seeing or talking to someone else. Well, I got there and, within the first hour of what was supposed to be a three-day trip, I found out he had been seeing someone for two weeks. Huh? Say what? So, not only was I too short that weekend, I found out he was taken.

Okay, God. I get it. Have you ever found yourself in a place where you really couldn't blame anyone but yourself? It wasn't God's fault I wasn't listening to Him. It was my fault. I didn't have the courage to listen to the Holy Spirit. Why? Because I didn't want to hear the answer and hear the truth of what was to come. I know you are reading this right now feeling the same way. We push things aside for a long time, hoping and praying what we feel deep down inside isn't the truth. More than likely, it is. I was devastated when he told me he was seeing someone else. Why? I don't know. I didn't want to hear it because I had invested time, money, and emotion in someone who in the end wanted nothing to do with me.

If you remember anything from this chapter please remember this: You are worth more than you are more than likely settling for right now. Finding someone who respects you isn't a fairy-tale love. You have to believe you are worth more. We attract what we feel inside about ourselves. It's not always the other person's fault. When you start to see your worth and value, then and only then do your eyes open to the truth. You then quit wasting your time on meaningless and purposeless relationships.

Don't stay in a one-sided relationship that is leaving you more exhausted than filled up.

Don't ever give up. Stand strong in your faith and know God has someone in mind just for you!

Chapter 15
Relationship 101

Don't keep beating yourself up. Grown, learn, and move on.

RECENTLY I HAD TO come to grips with just how hard relationships are sometimes. It doesn't matter what type of relationship it is, whether it is with family, friends, or someone you really like. I'll be the first to preach about relationships because I have had many experiences I have been able to learn and grow from. I believe God is putting me into this platform to reach out to hundreds and thousands of people to establish their worth and what they truly deserve. Note: I am not saying I am an expert. I'm only speaking from my heart, my experiences, and what I feel God has led me to write.

When it comes to discovering our worth, I also want to point out that it isn't always the other person's fault when things go south in a relationship. It so easy to point a finger, to blame, and to put it all on the other person, isn't it? Why would we ever want to sit back and look at ourselves? I'll tell you why: because typically a lot of pain is involved.

When change needs to happen within ourselves, pain is almost always involved. God is the potter and we are the clay.

Yet you, LORD, are our Father. We are the clay, you are the potter; we are all the work of your hand.
(Isaiah 64:8)

It is a constant molding process. So, every time change needs to happen we get that sick feeling in our stomach and sometimes pain that seems almost unbearable to deal with. This is why God brings people in our life for reasons and for seasons. It could be for the other person, but don't forget the lesson could also be for you.

Admitting when you are wrong doesn't make you a weak person. Saying sorry first doesn't mean the other person has control over you. Relationships today are based on lists. *You did this for me; I have to do this for you.* There is always a score being kept of rights and wrongs. In relationships we feel we have the right to be happy—almost as though the other person owes us something all the time. This is such a wrong way of thinking. Your relationship will fail if all you expect is the other person to make you happy all the time. It is a selfish act at that. Yes, you should be happy; I'm not saying you shouldn't. I am saying you need to check in with your own expectations of someone else and see if that person, in reality, can even meet any of them. In a world filled with technology, texts messages become a way of communication—communication that can be good and also that can be bad. We want instant gratification. When you text someone, you put the expectation on them that they need to text you back right away. When they don't meet that, you have already created 25,000 scenarios in your head as to why they haven't texted you back when only 30 minutes have gone by. Been there?

We lead more with selfishness than we do with love. Love, as in how you can serve the other person. Love, as in "What can I do for you to help make your day easier?" Whatever happened to lifting up the people in your life instead of making it all about you? I hear all the time how people wish they had more support from their spouse, family, and friends.

Our selfish acts can stem from pain we have experienced in the past. You become selfish because you say to yourself you will never be treated that way again. You've already made up in your mind that the next person you meet will serve you or else. *We truly forget our worth and also the worth of the other person.* We forget to walk in grace and forgiveness. If you want to hold a long-term relationship, then all the junk from your past cannot be constantly brought into your future relationships. You can't expect or assume the next person is going to treat you like the last one did. You could possibly ruin something good that you have for the first time in your life.

My point is that expectations can be dangerous. I'm not saying all expectations are bad. I'm simply trying to say that, through my own experiences, I see how I still tend to do this. We are not brought into this world being selfless. At a young age we constantly are saying "my toys," "my stuff," "my this or that." Everything when we are younger is always "mine." This is not the attitude we can have going into our relationships. We have to learn how to serve and how to lead with love for the other person. We have to learn how to not make it all about us all the time.

I really hope that today you can take a moment to reflect on your own relationships and ask yourself what you are bringing to the table. Are you helping or trying to make things easier for the other person, too? Are you lifting them up and pouring into them? What can you do today to improve your own relationships?

False Illusion: You Are Not Good Enough

The moment I saw his name pop up on my cell phone was the moment my heart started racing. At the end of 2014, I didn't want to read what was about to come next unless it was him telling me he wanted to be with me and that he just needed some time. Well, that wasn't the case. What it said was he wanted space, didn't want a serious relationship, and felt like he couldn't give me what I wanted. I stared at those words for what felt like forever. I sat down with my heart still racing as reality sank in that he no longer wanted to be with me. I sat longer. I reread those words over and over again. Earlier that week he'd said he was feeling overwhelmed and felt pressure from every area of his life. That just meant he needed some time, right? Not that he didn't want to be with me, right?

The longer I sat there and stared at those words in the text, the more pain I began to experience. As you've read throughout this book,

2014 wasn't exactly my best year for dating, and there I was getting told through a text that it was over. But I didn't want it to be over. I had so many things I wanted to say. More pain rushed throughout my entire body. I kept rereading those words as if another text was going to come through saying, "We can work things out." Unfortunately, that text never came. What followed were my own thoughts of "You are not good enough. You never were."

When I read that text message it was almost like it was saying or screaming to me, "I'm sorry. I can't fit you into my busy life. I need to spend time drinking and being with my friends. You wanting to see me is taking up that time, and I don't want to have to keep choosing." I knew his life was busy. What was screaming to me through that text could have had nothing to do with it at all. Maybe that wasn't the reason why he didn't want to be with me. All I wanted to do was help take the pressure off of him. I didn't want him to feel overwhelmed, especially by me. We kept saying, "Let's just get through football season and things will slow down." (He coaches seventh-/eighth-grade football.) Things ended, though, slightly before football season was over. It was the weekend before Sweetest Day and two weeks before my birthday. We had plans for the rest of the month, and my birthday was going to be a very special day. (What was up with guys wanting to break it off with me before special events were about to take place? Moving on…) I changed all my plans. I canceled everything. As a woman, an emotional being, I just couldn't keep the same plans—that I had planned to spend with him. It didn't feel right, and I didn't want to have to think about it more than I needed to. The pain cut deep because it felt like a never-ending battle of not being good enough. I just wanted to ask him, "Why wasn't I worth the fight? Why wasn't I worth the few nights a week? We barely saw each other and you wanted more space?"

Many would argue that it was only a little more than a two-month relationship—as if relationships and people are no big deal. Regardless of how long you are with someone, that should not ever determine a person's worth. They should still be treated with respect. *No matter what.* Granted, you cannot make someone see your worth, but it doesn't mean that you can't see theirs. I saw everything he could have been and was, but I don't think he ever saw it himself. I don't think he ever thought he deserved it, either. I wasn't perfect; I don't claim to be. I fell for someone who for the first time in a long time respected me.

I wasn't going to beg for him back. I don't want to try to persuade someone why they should be with me. (I learned my lesson earlier in 2014 with that one.) I was only hoping that he had seen my heart and that my intentions were to be supportive and lift him up. Believe it or not, I learned so much in such a short time about relationships. It was one of the biggest growth spurts I have had—but also one of the hardest.

Time for Healing

During the week following, after the breakup, I knew that I had a very long road ahead of me for recovering—not just from this particular relationship but from everything that had happened over time. God was opening me up and showing me everything that I needed to work on me. That's the key word: *me*. I was realizing some of the maturing I had to do when it came to relationships. God was showing me where I needed to start my relationships from. See, you are not out just looking for a significant other. You shouldn't just be saying, "This one looks good" and then hoping it works. It wasn't that I wasn't good enough. It was an illusion that the enemy wanted me to believe. Maybe he was brought into my life by God, for God, to help me learn a new lesson in life. Also, that can go the other way: Maybe I needed to be in his life for a lesson. It could be simpler, too: Maybe we just simply weren't supposed to be together. I love how God can use people or situations to actually redirect our paths. We fall off the path He wants us to be on only to find ourselves turned back onto the right path, by pain usually. Yes, pain is usually involved, because we get off the path by our own human fleshly desires. So, in order to redirect us like the gentle father He is, He gives us a little tough love. We want to blame God for the pain but we have to realize that God doesn't always put us in these situations. In fact, we usually put ourselves in them.

The story of Leah in the Bible is one I am sure a lot of us can relate to. I can't imagine having multiple children in the hope of being loved by a man.

> *When the LORD saw that Leah was not loved, he opened her womb, but Rachel was barren. Leah became pregnant and gave birth to a son. She named him Reuben, for she said, "It is because the LORD has seen my misery. Surely my husband will love me now." She conceived again, and when she gave birth to a son she said, "Because the LORD heard that I am not loved, he gave me this one too." So she named him Simeon. Again she conceived, and when she gave birth to a son she said, "Now at last my husband will become attached to me, because I have borne him three sons." So he was named Levi. She conceived again, and when she gave birth to a son she said, "This time I will praise the LORD." So she named him Judah. Then she stopped having children.*

(Genesis 29:31–35)

We do so many things to get noticed by someone. We give up our standards, we use our bodies, and we compromise our goals because we want to be loved. Instead of staying true to who we are, we allow someone else to form us that isn't God. Therefore, we end up miserable and unhappy. The story of Rachel and Leah goes back in forth in competition for love. Then it gets to the point where they are almost just in competition with each other with regard to who can have the most children. I just love this story in the Bible because I know a lot of people can relate to it. It's real. It shows just how imperfect we are but just how perfect His love is. It shows that Rachel and Leah were human and were not perfect, fighting for the love of a man when they should have been searching for God's heart even more. It was amazing, though, because God was there the whole time listening to them. Leah became aware that although she wasn't the focus of her husband's love she was loved by God. With her fourth pregnancy she drew nearer and nearer to God. From then on she began to praise God, knowing His love for her.

Can't you see how this relates?

We go through all kinds of trials. As we allow those trials to make us stronger and we become closer and closer to God, we realize He will always be who we need and who loves us, imperfections and all.

When we seek self-fulfillment we will end up miserable, have heartache, and end up in pain. As we draw closer to God each day we find our fulfillment in Him. He will then begin to remove the competition in our hearts, the insecurities, the jealousies, and the heartaches. Your true inner beauty will begin to grow and your heart will be at rest.

Chapter 16
Wake Up: Know Your Worth

Your time is now. It's not tomorrow or "one day." It's right now.

ON A DAILY BASIS I am faced with a harsh reality of what people have been through in their life. I would love to tell you that more than half were raised in such a way that they believe they could change the world, but it is just not the case. The reality for people I work with is that for most of their life someone told them that they were no good. They were told they would never be anyone or amount to anything. From being raped by their father to being mentally abused by their mother, it's a never-ending cycle of defeat. It's a never-ending cycle of abuse. It's a never-ending cycle of pain.

I want you to wake up right now and realize that your past does not have to become your reality. You don't need to settle for that man/woman who is treating you like you are just an accessory that they occasionally want to wear (*aka* be around). Let me insert a truth now that God says about you:

For we are God's masterpiece. He has created us anew in Christ Jesus, so we can do the good things He planned for us long ago.
(Ephesians 2:10)

You are His masterpiece. You are not identified by another person. The only person who identifies you is God. Relationships can be distractions that the enemy sends, or relationships can be blessings. Either way you have the opportunity to choose what you get out of a relationship that ends. You don't realize your worth in a day. Sometimes it takes multiple bad relationships before you realize the pattern that you fall into. I don't know if you even notice yourself, which is why I hope you are reading this book—so that your eyes are opened to maybe what your relationship really is and not what you think it is.

Most people going into a relationship have their "love blinders" on. They don't see past the things they like. They only focus on the good. When you have your blinders on, though, you don't see the reality of what really is. You start holding onto the few good things they may have done for you instead of seeing how the other person may really be treating you—which is typically like crap. Treating you like you are an option. Seeing you only when it is convenient for them. Get my drift? I am fully aware that life gives us complications and busy work schedules. I will always fully believe that if you are important to someone they will make time for you, whether in person, a phone call, or a simple text.

Stop playing around in relationships. Stop breaking your own heart because you want to be in a relationship for all the wrong reasons. Take loneliness, for example. That probably made you cringe a little because you know it's the truth. Far too often I hear about people being in a relationship just because they don't want to be alone. They pick up the first person they see who is cute and has some good qualities that they maybe can withstand over time. For women, since we are emotionally led human beings, it is easier to be swept off our feet by words. We ignore the actions because really there are none to back up the words. When this so-called "honeymoon phase" ends, reality sets in and you start to see who they really are, and you break up. Then once again, the cycle repeats itself.

Let's talk about this "honeymoon phase." Someone needs to crack this topic wide open. It was brought to my attention after talking with my spiritual dad that it doesn't really exist. It is made up by society—

made up by all the fairy-tale and love movies. The more I thought about it, the more I felt like it was true. See, we fall head over heels for someone. Our *feelings* take control, and we feel bliss—like life couldn't be any better. We choose not to see any flaws in the person and think they will change. Some may even think it is cute for a little while.

In the beginning, you don't really know each other, so the whole exploration thing is pretty exciting. It's like the first few months of your relationship are one big party or fairy tale because you both are learning about each other. It's all about the date nights, long hours staying up texting, and being spoiled with gifts and showered with attention. Then, well, things calm down. You don't see each other as much and you think something has changed. Date nights don't happen as often and you think the butterflies are gone. This person is no longer staying up for hours on end texting you. This person is no longer giving you the attention you once received. This is where the work comes. This is when you become selfless. This is where the relationship actually begins. See, most of the time when that "phase" is over, people want to give up on it. They think, "This person isn't doing this for *me* anymore so I am going to go and find someone who will." The person you started dating was always the same person. Yes, even six months later. (I know people can change for the better. That's not what I am talking about here.) You failed to see the things you really didn't like because you were hoping to change and mold them specifically for you.

Worth the Wait

I don't know too many people who love waiting. I mean, I hate waiting in a doctor's office. You make an appointment and then it seems like you wait three hours in the waiting room then wait again in the exam room. It's like you have to plan a whole day off just for a doctor's visit where you actually might only spend five minutes with the person. (Please note my sarcasm. I don't want any doctors or receptionists writing to me!) Waiting on an answer or waiting on a friend to call you back is just as annoying sometimes. We always want answers right now. We want an immediate response to our needs.

I see this all the time in relationships. I, too, got sick of waiting. So I did like everyone else tends to do: I settled for mediocre. We don't want to wait any longer. We think God has forgotten about us so we proceed to take things into our own hands. *God isn't going to bring it, so I'm going to force it to happen.* You probably know this by now, but this is a terrible plan. It's an awful plan that leads to more pain than we want to experience and more loneliness than we want to feel.

We need to have a different approach. We need a different mind-set regarding how we view our relationships. I have a lot of failed attempts. I have experienced pain that I don't want any of you to have to face. It's been a long journey for me, and I'm encouraging you to open your heart and allow me to speak to you. We all should have starting points when it comes to how we first engage with someone. We need to get past this whole "I'm just going to date to date" thing. If you want to be married, then just stop that mentality and save yourself money, time, and the emotional roller-coaster. Your starting points should stem from your own values, priorities, goals, and morals. You should know each other spiritually, emotionally, and mentally. You should know where each of you stands with regard to the most important areas of your life. When it comes down to your core values, you can't change someone to have the same ones as you do—nor should you settle and bypass those desires of your heart, just to maintain a relationship. *Must I say that if you don't know what you want, then you will in fact settle for anything that anyone gives you?* Then you will wonder why you are upset and unhappy all the time. You must establish where your worth comes from. Your worth comes from Christ. He sets the standards for your relationships and who you should be dating. He is your Father.

If you desire to marry a godly man/woman then why are you even considering someone who is far from it? Stop the nonsense. Check yourself and get your emotions under control. Are you just lonely? Are you searching for someone to fill you up all the time? Start to pray for your future spouse. Write letters to your future spouse. Ask God to give you the desires of your heart. More importantly, pray about wanting God's will for your life and not your own.

It's worth the wait, my friends, to finally be at peace with yourself without having to be with someone or just having someone there. When you find that peace you never know who God will bring into your life. God is good. He can bring someone into your life in the blink of an eye when you didn't see it coming. So, stop settling for mediocrity, and start praying and believing God for your blessing in that area.

Whenever I post something about loving other people, some of the same things said are: *How do I love someone who is constantly hurting me? How do I love someone who doesn't appreciate me or my love? Do I stay in my marriage and keep loving even when I am not respected?*

I don't have all the answers to those questions. I have never been married. Here is what I do have: my experiences.

Up until about two years ago I thought I was in love. Honestly, I think I was just in love with the idea of being in love. From a very young age I was taught to fend for myself, whether it was buying my own shampoo or buying my own bed, in my high school years. Fending for myself taught me "If I don't do this, then no one will. I can *only* rely on myself." Maybe you have felt like this a time or two—where you feel all the weight on your shoulders and know if you don't do it, it won't get done. If you don't mind me challenging you, how strong is your faith? Are you relying on God? Those were two questions that were asked to me last year. I had to ask myself if I was doing my part, then letting God do His. Was I living in faith or was I living trying to control everything? Last year was when I started to develop true love. God is true love. He is everything.

God is love, and he who abides in love abides in God, and God in Him.
(1 John 4:16)

We don't always see eye-to-eye, but He always has my best interest on His heart. Sometimes I don't want to listen but I know He loves me anyway. He is constantly nudging me in the right direction with sweet and gentle whispers. His voice is soft and without condemnation.

I want to love like Jesus.

This brings me back to my main topic: How do you love people who are hurting you? First, you need to take a step back and evaluate the relationship you are in. We can't point the finger if we never take a look at ourselves. I am *not* saying you deserve to be treated wrongly. Rather, I am asking: Are you allowing this to happen to you when you *know* you should have walked away? Time and time again when I speak with people about relationships they say they knew it wasn't going to work out but they stayed because they were comfortable and didn't want to deal with the breakup. So you are completely miserable but don't want to leave the relationship because you don't want to make them sad? More often than not, the answer to that question would be yes. Loving people can be shown by letting them go. By loving people enough to say, "This isn't healthy and maybe we need to both work on ourselves." Know your worth and their worth, too.

We should love every person we come in contact with, like Jesus would, through their struggles, difficulties, insecurities, and more. It doesn't always mean that we need to be close with them and put ourselves in a place of danger. We can pray for them. We can love them in many ways that are safe for both parties. Please note that I am not saying to run and get a divorce or leave a relationship you are in. Those of you reading who need to hear what I am saying know exactly who you are.

God Is Good

God changed me and the way I view love. I have shown love to people who I didn't think deserved it *at all*. But you know what? It is not about what I think people deserve. We all sin and make mistakes. We all upset people and made people mad. I really have to remember we are all God's children.

A sweet little reminder of loving people can be found in John 12:34–35:

A new command I give you: Love one another. As I have loved you, so you must love one another. By this everyone will know that you are my disciples, if you love one another.

Love sometimes means forgiving and letting go of years of hatred. You know right now in your heart what you need to work on or do. Don't be afraid to listen to what the Holy Spirit is saying to you right now. We need to start loving with intention and become less selfish.

Every day is a new opportunity to show someone love and appreciation. Are you using one of the greatest gifts God has given us?

Love is patient, love is kind. It does not envy, it does not boast, it is not proud. It does not dishonor others, it is not self-seeking, it is not easily angered, it keeps no record of wrongs. Love does not delight in evil but rejoices with the truth. It always protects, always trusts, always hopes, always perseveres. Love never fails.
(1 Corinthians 13:4–8)

Chapter 17
Soul Ties and Strongholds

When you give yourself to somebody you give more than just your body.
You give them a piece of your soul.

I HAVE BEEN STARING at the chapter title for some time now. To be honest, I have been putting off writing this chapter for a few weeks. This is a topic not too many people I know even talk about. It's a topic I have struggled with my whole life.

I'm hoping to share why you might have such strong feelings for someone even though they may have treated you like crap. I'm hoping to answer why it is so hard to get over someone you know you should have never been with in the first place. I'm hoping that you can find peace knowing why you may feel so lost, lonely, and depressed.

As you have read, I didn't know God all my life. I started my relationship with Him when I was in my early 20s. Being clueless to what real love was and clueless to what a real relationship was led me to make many wrong decisions in my life. I made a lot of decisions based on feelings and emotions. The decisions were based on acceptance. I wanted someone to love me. I thought one way to get someone to love me was to have sex with them. In search for validation I discovered more pain. In search for happiness, joy, and peace I discovered lies, rumors, and cheating. It's so hard to feel full when everything you try to do to fill you up makes you feel even emptier inside. I wondered: *Was I always going to feel this way? When was I going to feel full? When was I no longer going to need the things of the world to make me happy inside?*

What Is a Soul Tie?

The Bible speaks of what is today known as soul ties. The Bible doesn't use the word *soul tie,* but it speaks of soul ties when it talks about souls being knit together, becoming one flesh, etc. A soul tie can serve many functions, but in its simplest form, it ties two souls together in the spiritual realm. Soul ties between married couples draw them together, whereas soul ties between non-married people can draw an abused woman to a man from whom, in the natural realm, she would hate and run from, but instead she runs to him even though he doesn't love her and treats her like dirt. In the demonic world, unholy soul ties can serve as bridges between two people to pass demonic things through. Other soul ties can do things such as allow one person to manipulate and control another person, with the other person unaware of what is going on, or knowing what is going on but, for no real reason, allowing it to continue.

I have had the pleasure of being able to work with a lot of married women. Even in marriage one person or both people can bring in different demonic spirits together that may be traveling through doors left open throughout their family history. So I know it is not just for those who are not married. You create a soul tie with whomever you engage sexually.

Sex today is just more casual. It is for pleasure. Most of the time it stems from lust rather than love. There are way too many feelings in the beginning of a relationship that we push to the side in order to get what we want right now: satisfaction, validation, approval, to feel loved and cared for—and the list goes on. *This person, I know, really cares about me because they have sex with me even though they never make time for me other than when they are ready for more. They have to care, right? That person means so much to me even though that person abuses me in every way, shape, and form but they care because we sleep in bed together. That person wouldn't just have sex with me if they didn't care.* I was wrong—so wrong.

Sex causes a lot of lines to be blurred in a relationship. Sex is great. Sex is awesome. God created it, so of course it has to be something amazing. The thing is, though, sex is the wrong starting point for a relationship.

Blurry Lines

The number of kids having sex and engaging in foreplay scares me. I feel like it is only getting worse as the years go on. It also seems like kids are younger and younger when they start being sexually active with someone else. I hear parents say all the time that their kid wouldn't do such a thing. I hear stories about how they will make it impossible for them to do that. I'm not a parent—I understand that—but I can give you the other side: If someone wants to have sex or engage in foreplay, they will do almost anything to do just that. No matter how much someone tries to stop them or prevent it, there is almost always a way around it. So, instead of trying to be controlling and locking them in their room or a straitjacket, I suggest educating your children. I only say that because I wish I would have had a loving, tender, caring parent speaking into my life every chance they had. I also know that you could do everything in your power as a parent and do all "the right things," and things still go wrong. I hope more than anything you can feel my passion for this topic.

I was never educated about the side of sex where your soul is connected with someone else's. I didn't grow up in a spiritual Christian home. I think my parents knew I was having sex, but it was never addressed in a way that was informative and showed that they cared. Sex is so much more than just the physical pleasure you feel for a short duration of time. It allows your soul to be opened up with another person. That means if their soul is full of garbage, then you get that garbage, too. This goes for sex and foreplay. Any kind of sexual act will connect you with the other person. Sex is barely talked about, and when it is everyone kind of shies away from it. It's like everyone is embarrassed to talk about it. I think that's the problem. Sex isn't an unnatural thing for people to do. Like I said, God created it for two people—*but* for two married people to be in covenant with each other.

That is why a man leaves his father and mother and is united to his wife, and they become one flesh.
(Genesis 2:24)

If you would have asked me a year ago if I was going to wait until I got married to have sex I probably would have said absolutely not—yes, just a year ago. The great thing about God is that He gives us grace. I am able to have a second chance. If I mess up, He will be there for my third chance as well. Messing up shouldn't just purposely happen, though. Each time should be a renewing of your mind, spirit, and soul. It should be about moving forward from the last mistake.

I have become so passionate about this topic because I was so sick, broken, wounded, crushed, and weak for so many years. I gave my body to men. I gave my soul to men. I gave my heart to men. Being single now and going through one of the roughest seasons of my life, I am finally beginning to walk in freedom after 15 years of bondage, strongholds, and soul ties.

At the very young age of 12 I lost my virginity. I was at an age where I should be hanging out with my friends, playing outside, and just be a 12-year-old little girl. Nope, not me. I was out on the search for men. I was in sixth grade, going into seventh. I remember my first time with foreplay as well. I remember where I was, who I was with, and how I felt. It was uncomfortable and weird, and I thought, "Why am I doing this?" I had absolutely no clue what I was doing. Becoming pregnant never even entered my thought process. I don't even know if knew how to conceive at that age and point in my life. I had no business doing what I was doing, but nothing inside of me was telling me that I was doing something wrong—well, nothing that I knew to listen to, I guess you could say. Once that door opened, it stayed open.

I was just a kid who thought she was going to be broke, living with merely nothing, for the rest of her life. I had no goal other than to find someone to be with who would love me. This continued into high school. My identity became more and more strongly associated with men. I didn't realize that every time I slept with a boyfriend, my soul was being crushed and opened up to new spirits. Whatever their spirit was entered into mine, and we became one. It doesn't just happen when you get married. It happens anytime you engage with someone that way. Time and time again I allowed this to happen. *Oh, look, someone likes me. I better sleep with him so I know he cares and he loves me. I better make sure to keep him happy so he doesn't go and like someone else.* If the only reason you are sleeping with someone is fear of them going and finding/getting it from someone else, then you never had them in the first place. Ouch! I know that is probably tough to read, but let's keep it real. God didn't create sex to keep your half-time, sometime, maybe-time, if-I-have-time person around; He created it to be special between two married people.

If you have this kind of attitude right now, I hope you take a moment to step back and realize how precious your body and soul are. I pray you start taking this more seriously. I pray that you look at your body in a whole new light—not something you just give away because someone likes your muscles or curves. You are so much more than that. In fact, I bet some of you wish people saw beyond just your body and looks.

Be encouraged by scripture to know the value of your body and just how precious you are.

Therefore, I urge you, brothers and sisters, in view of God's mercy, to offer your bodies as a living sacrifice, holy and pleasing to God—this is your true and proper worship. Do not conform to the pattern of this world, but be transformed by the renewing of your mind. Then you will be able to test and approve what God's will is—his good, pleasing and perfect will.
(Romans 12:1–2)

Do you not know that your bodies are members of Christ himself? Shall I then take the members of Christ and unite them with a prostitute? Never!

Do you not know that he who unites himself with a prostitute is one with her in body? For it is said, "The two will become one flesh." But whoever is united with the Lord is one with him in spirit. Flee from sexual immorality. All other sins a person commits are outside the body, but whoever sins sexually, sins against their own body. Do you not know that your bodies are temples of the Holy Spirit, who is in you, whom you have received from God? You are not your own; you were bought at a price. Therefore honor God with your bodies.
(1 Corinthians 6:15–20)

Don't you know that you yourselves are God's temple and that God's Spirit dwells in your midst? If anyone destroys God's temple, God will destroy that person; for God's temple is sacred, and you together are that temple.
(1 Corinthians 3:16–17)

Please know I am not here to bash or hate upon everyone who is having sex before marriage. I was there for a very long time. My goal isn't to make someone feel bad about their choices. I am here to help people discover their worth, what they deserve, and how they should be treated.

I actually thought I could get away with engaging in foreplay but not having sex. I made an agreement with myself that I would still get some sexual pleasure out of a relationship, but it wasn't as bad because I was still keeping my promise about not having sex. I broke the first promise with God after I was prayed over. I asked God for forgiveness and a second chance. I haven't broken that promise. I simply just bargained with God that I wouldn't have sex and convinced myself that foreplay was good and A-okay.

That being said, I was still very wrong. I don't know what God has been putting on your heart or what you are going through; I can only speak for myself and hope my message inspires you. Even though I didn't have sex and just engaged in foreplay, it has still been just as hard to move on and get over certain people. My last relationship tore me apart in that sense. I felt a deep, strong connection with him. Very deep. I cared for him, liked him, and wanted to share that intimacy with him. When I did, it obviously felt good, but the whole time I neglected my spirit saying, "God wants you to love yourself and your body." I neglected the fact that he didn't have a close relationship with the Lord and thought things would still be okay. I neglected the signs that kept popping up because deep down I knew he wasn't the guy that I was going to marry. He was a great guy. I know he had so much love to give and he didn't treat me horribly. Like I said before, I have nothing bad to say about him because God used him to teach me a lot about myself and what I still had to work on.

Since I neglected what I was feeling and since the relationship ended, it has been that much harder for me to get over him—harder for me to move on. Finally, I realized that for how passionate I am, I can't bring even foreplay into a relationship because the soul tie is just as strong. God allowed in His wisdom what He could have easily prevented. I had to go through the heartbreak. I had to experience this pain—only this time I was able to see how easily I was slipping into my old ways and using my body to feel something again. To fill a hole that I knew only Jesus could fill. Insecurities were brought forward; feelings I never knew I had before came to light all because of a connection I had with someone for all the wrong reasons.

For a very long time I felt like the woman at the well. If you are not familiar with this story, let me share it so you can have a better understanding:

Now he had to go through Samaria. So he came to a town in Samaria called Sychar, near the plot of ground Jacob had given to his son Joseph. Jacob's well was there, and Jesus, tired as he was from the journey, sat down by the well. It was about noon. When a Samaritan woman came to draw water, Jesus said to her, "Will you give me a drink?" (His disciples had gone into the town to buy food.) The Samaritan woman said to him, "You are a Jew and I am a Samaritan woman. How can you ask me for a drink?" (For Jews do not associate with Samaritans.) Jesus answered her, "If you knew the gift of God and who it is that asks you for a drink, you would have asked him and he would have given you living water."

*"Sir," the woman said, "you have nothing to draw with and the
well is deep. Where can you get this living water? Are you greater
than our father Jacob, who gave us the well and drank from it
himself, as did also his sons and his livestock?" Jesus answered,
"Everyone who drinks this water will be thirsty again, but whoever
drinks the water I give them will never thirst. Indeed, the water
I give them will become in them a spring of water welling up to
eternal life." The woman said to him, "Sir, give me this water
so that I won't get thirsty and have to keep coming here to draw
water." He told her, "Go, call your husband and come back." "I
have no husband," she replied. Jesus said to her, "You are right
when you say you have no husband. The fact is, you have had five
husbands, and the man you now have is not your husband. What
you have just said is quite true."*

(John 4:4–18)

When God is referring to the woman at the well having many
husbands, I don't view it as her literally being married to five men. I
view it more like she has slept with five men and is messing around
with men. Then He calls her out: *"and the man you now have is not
your husband."* Ouch! If you don't handle constructive criticism very
well, then I can see how this would make you feel a little uneasy inside.
When you can't handle legitimate constructive criticism from someone
who cares about you deeply, it is time to check your own heart. I'm
sure you know that person is telling you the truth, and speaking from
their heart, but you don't want to listen to it because dealing with it
may cause even more pain. I understand, but there is nothing better
than His love covering you and protecting you.

I don't look at it and say, "God, how mean." I look at that and say,
"God, thank you for loving me so much." I have had so many signs I
prayed for—situations in which I knew that a particular guy wasn't for
me—*but* as you can imagine I never listened to any of it. I would pray
for signs, get one, and then dismiss it. I'm pretty sure God was tired of
me having these long, drawn-out relationships over the years that He

would start to end them for me this year—hence me being broken up with every single time. His love is good and I know that without the little push from Him I would be stuck in a relationship, miserable, and not fulfilling the purpose He has called for me. Then I would end up married to someone who was only there to fill a void in the first place.

I challenge you to pray right now for your relationship or future relationship. Ask God to peel away layers and develop you into the person He has called you to be. This is a choice and a decision that you have to make—a necessary one. Stop hopping into bed with people just because your flesh desires to do so. You will always end up empty and alone in that bed when all is said and done, even if the person is next to you. Stop trying to force relationships that should have never happen and that you know won't work. Forcing will lead to failing. Save yourself heartbreak, protect your heart, and most importantly let God tend to your heart.

You are made for more than you are settling for right now.

Stop wasting your time on people who see absolutely no value in you.

Stop wasting your time going back to people and begging/bribing them to be with you.

Stop wasting your time trying to convince people you deserve better.

Stop wasting your time trying to change someone else to fit your mold.

Chapter 18
My Rainbow

Your happy ending is coming. It's time for God standards.

THERE IS NOTHING MORE beautiful than seeing a rainbow after a terrible storm. It is kind of like you almost forget about the storm and what just happened. You think about how something so amazing can happen after something so terrible. You can never see the ends of the rainbow, either. You want to believe that it keeps going. Rainbows do eventually disappear. Their beauty is left in our minds and hearts, and is never forgotten. Calm follows the rainbow until the next storm decides to pass through. The storm always tends to last longer than the rainbow, but we almost always know a rainbow is coming.

I love how God uses a rainbow to describe His connection with us:

I have set my rainbow in the clouds, and it will be the sign of the covenant between me and the earth. Whenever I bring clouds over the earth and the rainbow appears in the clouds, I will remember my covenant between me and you and all living creatures of every kind. Never again will the waters become a flood to destroy all life. Whenever the rainbow appears in the clouds, I will see it and remember the everlasting covenant between God and all living creatures of every kind on the earth. So God said to Noah, "This is

*the sign of the covenant I have established between me and all life
on the earth."*

(Genesis 9:13–17)

Again I am reminded how good His love is. He calms the storms.
His love and beauty always will shine through even in the midst of the
clouds, reminding me that He never leaves me.

Can you see how life flows through calmness, storms, and then
rainbows? We get so caught up in the storms that we forget the good
that is coming—the lesson to be learned. We don't even want to
search for a blessing in a burden because we pity ourselves with this
whole "Why me?" bologna. We stay in seasons way longer than we
ever should because of it. I knew that sometime soon my rainbow was
going to come—that all the pain I have felt over the years wasn't going
to be for nothing. My biggest weakness—men and relationships—has
turned into one of my greatest strengths. Even in the midst of my
lonely seasons I knew God had something bigger for me, even if I never
acted like it. I had so many moments where I didn't want to proceed.
I didn't want to put up a fight anymore. I was done feeling pain. I
couldn't understand why no one wanted to be with me. I hit such a
really low point in my life. It felt almost unbearable at times. If God
didn't give me the people I needed in my life, then I really don't know
where I would be.

After my last breakup I knew a very new season was upon me—a
season in which I was going to rejoice in everything and be content
with whatever I had. I knew I had a desire in my heart to be married,
but I wasn't willing to just marry anyone who crossed my path and
wanted to date me. After I was able to mend and get over that, for
the first time I was at peace in my soul. It took some weeks to be able
to control my thoughts about things—to come to terms with reality.
When I did, I knew I had changed. It is something so indescribable.
It runs deep within you and it consumes you. It is all God and His
workings. I remember saying to God that I didn't want anything that
wasn't a part of His will for my life. I refused to embark on another

journey without His take on it first. If God didn't approve, or the instant I felt discernment, it was no more. The standards rose to God standards, and I wasn't going back or settling for less. I couldn't. It was not an option. A new season was there, and I was in my rainbow.

Someone My Soul Desires

I don't know if there is ever just one person out there for us, like a "soul mate." I think God can work wonders bringing people together. What if you didn't marry your "one"? That means you screwed up the whole pattern of someone else's "one." You get my point. For a long time I was really aiming at nothing. I always went by looks first, then everything else. Finding a "one" for me seemed like an impossible task until I started praying about being the "one" for someone else. I really started to shift my thinking and how I viewed relationships. I knew it wasn't just about the other person making me happy. There is so much more about a relationship than our own selfish desires guiding us. It takes work. More importantly, it takes work on yourself. I started really praying for my future husband. I had a list, actually. Here is what some of my list looked like (not in any particular order):

- Has to have a passion in some way for health and fitness
- Knows who he is and where he is going in life
- God #1 in his life
- Be my #1 one biggest supporter
- Compliments me, calms me down, and keeps me in check with my priorities
- Has passion
- Isn't intimidated by my success and can grow with me knowing who he is
- Wants to travel the world, too
- Tall
- Muscular build

- Good sense of style

- Makes me laugh

- A giver—a generous giver

- Would do missions with me

- Accepts me for everything I am and am not

That was some of my list. Yes, I did have some superficial requirements. I love taller men, so why not write that down and talk to God about it? He wants to give me all the desires of my heart; I truly believe that. Some people made fun of the list, and I actually didn't care. I really wanted to know what I was looking for in a man. What are you looking for in your significant other? Are you setting standards? Do you even know what makes you happy and what doesn't? Do you really think God doesn't want to provide you with someone you are meant to be with? I don't think so. That's when we come into the picture. We need to be able to discern our own relationships and go from there. God doesn't always bring someone into your life who you are supposed to marry. Sometimes the enemy uses people to get to us.

Relationships can be big lessons if they go further than they should. This is why I started to set the God standards and started praying for my future husband. I actually would talk to him throughout the day and tell God to bless him. I spent time writing letters to him when I was having a rough day, knowing he was out there waiting to meet me, too. The closer I drew to the Lord, the stronger I felt about it. The closer I drew the more discernment I had for the people I would start talking to. Sometimes it wouldn't even get past a few conversations before I knew it wasn't going to go anywhere. That's how close I was with God. I would just feel "Nope, he's not the one." It went all the way down to the little details. If I saw he was only 5' 5", then I just knew he wasn't the one. I was pretty serious about wanting a taller man, around 6 feet. Call me crazy, but God cares about the little details just as much! Looking at my list and saying I wouldn't date anyone shorter seems pretty selfish and unnecessary, and I get that. I used to be the same way when people would tell me specific things. I would think, "You are crazy and not going to find what you want." I had strong desires in my heart for specific requests. I never hesitated to ask for them. I believed so deeply about it all.

My Miracle

I used to tell people to not be so picky. They would say things they really wanted to have in a significant other, and I sometimes said, "You may have to have grace for them in that area," and so on. It was almost like I was telling them to settle for less because I was also struggling to find someone who had my goals, values, and beliefs. I had never really had it, so I thought maybe you have to do a lot of compromising when it comes to finding someone to love. When I say *compromising,* I am more referring to the details I wanted. By world standards and views, to have specific desires is almost unheard of. It's like people will take anything and be miserable. People are more in pain being with someone than they would be alone. I see it all the time: They stay, thinking things are going to change—thinking the other person is going to change. The crazy, cool thing about God, though, is that He can change us if we allow Him to. He can bring someone into our life who we never saw coming. We just have to have faith in His timing.

Moving Forward...

Have you ever met someone with cancer or who has recovered from it? Recently I did. It was the first time I had ever really known a cancer patient. I believe my grandma had cancer, but I was so young and too disconnected from my family to remember. My other grandma had melanoma. I never really experienced a close relationship with someone who had, let alone survived, cancer. Every time I hear this man tell his story it brings tears to my eyes. He had a very rare form of testicular cancer. His prognosis was 20- to 30-percent survival. Yet, every time he tells his story he speaks about it with such confidence. Before he went into the doctor's office, he pretty much knew he had cancer. He says he could just tell and feel it in his spirit. The night he realized he had it, he said he prayed with such clarity for the first time in his life, and he knew that everything was going to be okay. I think at that moment I knew he was my miracle. I don't know too many people who, in the face of trials, give it to God and fully believe it is going to be okay. We pray but then the worry overtakes us. The worry brings us down and makes us even sicker. When we pray and give it to God, that is exactly what we need to do. *Give it to God.* We need to rest while He does a work in us. That is exactly what He did with my miracle, Jon. Jon prayed for God to heal him but also said, "Whatever you want to happen, let it be your will for me. If I only have six months to live then let it be the best six months." He had to endure many chemo treatments. They left him very tired, but he prayed to God to not get sick or puke during them—and he never did. He actually made it to the gym about three or four times a week, even if it was only to get on the elliptical for 15 minutes.

Listening to Jon tell his story reminds me how faithful God is. This may not be the case for everyone, but it also reminds me how special each and every one of our lives is. We all have a special purpose in this world. You have a mission until God decides to take you home. It wasn't Jon's time yet. If you are reading this, then it is not your time yet. It is time for you to start living. Stop just hanging by a thread waiting to be cut. God wants to do a work in you, but you have to step up and show up in your own life.

Miracles happen every day, but it is our choice whether or not to believe in them.

My Perspective Got Me Closer

Everyone loves a great ending and a magical, fairy-tale love story. I hope my story inspires you to save yourself for someone God has planned for you. Your love story may not look like mine, but with God your love story will be better than you ever imagined or planned. When God is the center of it all, it will almost seem too good to be true. Other people will never be able to understand from a worldly perspective. You will have to fight the enemy off multiple times from trying to sever something beautiful that God has given you.

As I have talked about relationship after relationship, you can see the progression of how my point of view changed. With each relationship I found a new strength I didn't know I had—or that it even existed. When I started to pray to God for a man to come into my life, it was one of the most freeing things I ever did, because I no longer wanted to have control over it. I was so over the control of trying to find and hunt down someone—anyone—to be with me. I began to believe so deeply that God was working in my life to bring someone along who would "sweep me off my feet." The closer I drew to God, the more I knew it was all about His timing. When you go through breakup after breakup you instantly want to give up hope and throw your hands in the air. I almost did that multiple times but I was persistent in believing God had a plan for my love life.

From a worldly perspective, things like having someone who respects you, treats you well, and wants to nurture your relationship all at the same, become nonexistent. So, people tend to settle for maybe one of those, if any, because they don't think it will ever happen for them. They think that people are just "lucky" to find someone who treats them well.

Let me explain *worldly* a little bit more. I think that there is a "godly perspective" and a "worldly perspective." Most people I come in contact with are transformed by this world and others' opinions. There is no deep-rooted love with God in their lives. They are not striving to become better people. They settle for comfort and the thought that "This is always how it is going to be." They have a victim mind-set and believe that everyone always owes them something. They do not believe in forgiveness, only in retaliation. They do not believe in love, only the idea of love. The list goes on. The most important aspect of a worldly perspective is that we allow other people to determine our course instead of God. This is why we settle for mediocre relationships. This is why we live with anger, bitterness, and resentment. Very few people truly want to see you happy and will encourage you along the way, no matter what you are going through. They always want the best for you, and not out of their own selfish desires, either.

When you have a godly perspective, then your whole view about life changes. You start to see things the way God would see them. You start to love like you have never loved before. Your heart breaks free from all the things that have been holding you down. You see people differently. Most importantly, your relationships are completely changed. My goal is to be more and more like God every day. I want to love like He loves. I want to walk out my faith with courage and bravery like He did. The list is never-ending. Although I am not perfect, His love is perfect. So, when it came to me finding someone for me, I knew He had a perfect love for me. I am His daughter and He wouldn't want me to just be with anyone. As relationships passed I knew that God was pushing me along. When I dated someone He would make things end pretty quickly, almost as if He were saying to me, "Jess, you had the choice to walk away and didn't, so now I am just speeding up the process for you." It was always in a loving way. No more long-term relationships that were not going anywhere. No more just being in a relationship to have someone there and feed my loneliness. That was all over. It was time for a new beginning.

God Is the Ultimate Matchmaker

Many people I know are against online dating sites. They think they're creepy and weird, and they believe that God will bring someone into their life by them simply not doing anything. I'm not saying you have to join a dating site, but at least go out to new places and meet new people every week. Many say they don't want to spend hours on a computer talking with people and would rather meet in person. I can see both perspectives, especially today, when anyone can create a fake profile and pretend to be someone they are not. For me, though, I was all for it. I thought it was rather exciting to have options and to not have to worry about the awkward, sit-down date where you barely know anything about the other person except the fact that they may be attractive. I like being able to read something about someone and going from there. Not everyone may share my perspective, and that is completely okay. I have dated in person, gone on dates suggested by friends, and also joined a dating site. Many people laugh about joining one. They think the sites are for people who are unattractive, can't find dates, or are losers. That is so *not* the case. To be honest, I was sick of dealing with the people I was dating, and was ready for something new and different. It was kind of like an adventure to me.

Here's how I first joined a dating site: A girlfriend and I were reading a book together, and at one point it challenged us to join a dating website. I was for it; she was not. So, I joined for free and just checked things out. I signed up with the hope of maybe finding someone, or at least bringing hope back into my dating life. I wanted to believe that there were good godly men in this world. Up to that point I had never really experienced a man after God's own heart. I felt like I was fully practicing what I was preaching and God put me in check with that. I was all excited at first, and then I would get distracted by going on a date with someone local or falling for someone I knew. For months I continued with my free membership, though I don't think I ever really logged in but a few times here and there. The e-mails continued, only for me to delete them, thinking, "Maybe this is a waste of time." When I finally hit my breaking point, which you read about earlier, I knew I needed something different. I didn't want someone local in my small town where everyone knew everyone. I wanted to be able to have a fresh perspective and a new attitude going in.

That being said, I finally hit a very good season in my life. I had a long season of terrible dating from October 2013 to October 2014. I knew going into November that it was different. I used to not really enjoy the holiday season that much. It always brought up memories and things I didn't want to think about. I was always alone, and that wasn't what I wanted, either. For the first time in a very long time, if ever, 2014 was the first year my heart hit peace with everything. I remember watching one of the first snowfalls out of my kitchen window. The snow was coming down so slow and light, and it was beautiful.

I felt in my heart that this new season was going to be my best yet. I was content with being single. I was content with where I was in my life and who I was becoming for the first time in my life. I had the closest relationship with the Lord that I had ever felt, and peace just overcame my entire being. It was such an indescribable feeling. I wasn't going to settle for anything less than God had planned for me. I was ready to set new goals. Nothing was going to slow me down. I was on a mission to become the best me possible for God and for my future husband. That was my focus. Contentment.

After I hit that feeling, I felt like it was time to get back onto the dating site and actually pay for it. You're probably thinking, "You said you were content being single." I was for sure, but since I work from home, I enjoyed browsing people from all over and making new connections from the comfort of my living room after a long day of work. It just worked for me. I prayed about it before I paid for it. At that time the site was running a great deal, and I sat on it for a few days. *Do I really want to do this? Am I following what God wants me to do?* I kept asking myself these questions before I finally committed to paying for it. When you pay for it you can actually see what everyone looks like and so on. So, I would go on the site at night and just look around. I answered some questions people sent and also sent some questions to people, just building connections to see if it would even go anywhere. One day, a Thursday, after only having my membership for about a week, one guy stood out to me the most. He had asked me some questions, and I was intrigued. He was so handsome and, well, his profile wasn't amazing but the conversation kept flowing. Two days into our connection he gave me his number, which I was very hesitant about. I thought, "This guy has to be fake or desperate, one of the two." Holding nothing back, I went for it. I had nothing to lose and thought to myself, "If he is a crazy then I can just change my number." The risk, though, is something I felt I was willing to take. He met some of my requirements early on, and that is what kept it going. He was driven, was ambitious, set goals for himself all the time, and was an entrepreneur; his faith was strong; and the list goes on.

I texted him that night with an open mind. It was Saturday, only two days after we had initially started talking. He sent me one text back saying he would text me later and that he had a very busy day. The night went on and he didn't text me back. The next day I didn't hear from him until late afternoon. I already chalked it up to "whatever" at that point. He sounded great and amazing, but I wasn't going to let it bother me. I again became at peace because God is good. I wasn't hounding him with texts. There was no begging for him to talk to me or asking why he never texted me back until late the next day. I just had an "I don't care" attitude.

After we started talking on that Sunday, the conversation never stopped. We wanted to know everything about the other person. Both of us went in guns blazing because we didn't want to mess around anymore. We both wanted to find someone, but we weren't going to settle anymore. It was question after question, and answer after answer, when we realized we have a ton in common: his walk with his faith, view on children, goals, priorities, values, beliefs, etc. He wanted to talk on the phone Monday night. He was just as apprehensive as I was. Our first phone call was four and a half hours. Our second phone call was five hours. Our third phone call was five and a half hours. I think you can see where this is going. That week went so fast, as we talked every night after work into the wee hours of the morning. We never skipped a beat, and there was never any awkward silence. It was as though our souls had known each other forever but our flesh finally decided to meet. We were intentionally trying to weed out the other person in the beginning. With the intention of weeding him out and moving on to the next, my heart began to fall for him. It was the complete opposite of what I had planned. Words like *love* started to pop back up into my vocabulary—words I hadn't thought about using for a very long time.

When I broke up with the last boyfriend I had said "I love you" to, more than two years ago, I promised myself and felt it in my spirit that I was not going to tell someone I loved him until I knew he was the one I was going to marry. I had tossed around the word *love* way too much, and for the first time I wanted it to mean something.

Love isn't just a word or a feeling. It is just a powerful act and decision you decide to make every day in your relationships.

We talked about things that most couples never talk about right away. We dove into every topic possible to cover all the grounds of elimination. Of course, he wasn't going to be perfect, and neither was I. That wasn't the point. Our point was to make sure the most important things lined up. We spent hours getting to know each other without ever seeing each other face-to-face. We started to fall in love with each other because of our minds, not because of our physical features or bodies.

After a week of talking, we set a date to meet, in a bigger city, about an hour and a half away from me. He set up my hotel accommodations and took very good care of me. I was skeptical. I had had a lot of guys say something, but then their actions would never follow through. This was sort of my expectation going in with him as well. He sounded great and amazing—and really too good to be true.

Too good to be true? Why? Because I was always so used to dating people below my standards. Below what God intended for me. Below what my goals, morals, and beliefs were. Maybe you know exactly what I am talking about.

The Day We Met

My heart was pounding as I pulled into the hotel parking lot. I knew it was just moments before I would see the person with whom I felt like I was going to spend the rest of my life. Words can't really describe the feeling. Yes, I had seen pictures of him. In the back of my head, though, I couldn't help but think maybe it was a fake account and that some completely different person would be standing before me. I got out of my car and walked toward the revolving doors like he said to. It was almost something that you would see in a movie. As I got closer to the revolving doors, my eyes were poking around at everything I could see inside. I didn't see him at first, and then when I finally looked straight ahead, I saw him sitting down. Walking through the revolving doors that day completely changed my life. As soon as his eyes met mine he started walking toward me. We met in the middle, both with a sigh of relief and with a simple, nervous hug.

Our lives were forever changed that weekend.

We walked the city, got coffee and tea, and talked for hours upon hours. We walked through the park and sat on a bench that overlooked a beautiful river. On our second date he told me he loved me. It was a bold move. Out of my disbelief at first my only reaction to that was "Awww"—followed by "I love you, too." Never in my life have I ever said that on a second official date. People would think we were crazy and that it was all just emotions, but we begged to differ.

See, in our 20-some odd hours of talking on the phone before we met, we had covered a lot of topics, from hobbies and sports to views on marriage and kids. We covered everything: how we handle fights, our love languages, our beliefs, our goals, and so much more. We didn't want to waste time with someone who wasn't for us. As time went on we realized we were meant for each other. I dug through my old journal trying to find my "list" of what I wanted my dream guy to be like. I also found my goals of what I wanted to achieve. One goal specifically was "To witness a miracle of your healing power. To see you, God, come to life before me." God is so cool, because when I wrote that, he was going through his chemo treatments. It was almost like I was praying for him, and neither one of us knew. I never, ever wrote that goal again. It was only in that month on that one specific day.

Our process to eliminate each other only brought us closer than ever before. Our flesh may have just met, but our souls have known each other forever. He is my miracle. He is the cancer patient I talked about earlier, and I feel like God saved him just for me.

I knew during the second phone call that I was falling in love with him—a different kind of love. A deeper love. Only a love that God can understand. God is and always will be the ultimate matchmaker.

A Time for Everything

There is a time for everything, and a season for every activity under heaven: a time to be born and a time to die, a time to plant and a time to uproot, a time to kill and a time to heal, a time to tear down and a time to build, a time to weep and a time to laugh, a time to mourn and a time to dance, a time to scatter stones and a time to gather them, a time to embrace and a time to refrain, a time to search and a time to give up, a time to keep and a time to throw away, a time to tear and a time to mend, a time to be silent and a time to speak, a time to love and a time to hate, a time for war and a time for peace.

(Ecclesiastes 3:1–8)

Work on You

I believed that I always got better at relationships the more I had. I started to really think I had this one nailed, and then realized I am far from nailing anything. In our hope to be the best person to our significant other, we end up sometimes being the most selfish person we know. When you enter into a relationship with someone you think you are going to marry, I want to encourage you regarding a few things, so that you don't make the same mistakes *or* so that you are more aware for yourself.

When you are in a relationship with someone you will eventually commit your life to, you have to actually talk about things that will be fruit-producing in the relationship further on down the road. Differences need to be agreed upon and things need to be addressed— your spirituality, your view on money, your personality differences, and how you were raised, to name a few. These will all play a part in your future relationship with your significant other.

I finally buckled down and said, "I am going to learn to be the best partner and wife I can be. Can it really be that hard?" My personality is one that craves personal development. I always want to fix myself and make myself a better person. Little did I know just how much work I had left to do inside of me and how much I will always continue to have with each new season. How to learn to let the little things go, how you don't have to always prove your point, how you need to accept that the person you are with is completely different from you, and so on— these are the things I started to notice in myself that I needed to work on. Even after all the relationships I have been in and all the things I have learned in them, I realized that working on a relationship is a daily job in itself. I don't mean "job" in a negative way, but you do have to show up every day in your relationship. You have to make the effort. You have to put 100 percent of yourself forward. You have to be willing to do things even if they may not get noticed. You have to do the things that you might not even like because you know they're the right things to do. What keeps us showing up is our love for the other person. The choice we make every day is to commit to this one person.

Every day make a conscious effort to become selfless. If your goal is to have a long-lasting relationship, then you have to be willing to become selfless on a regular basis. Dating life will look a lot different from marriage life. But dating life will be a huge set-up for how married life will go. Marriage doesn't fix things. It will only enhance what you already are. Marriage will enhance the relationship you have built— just like having a ton of money doesn't change you; it only enhances who you are. The biggest thing we need to pay attention to is where our heart is in all that we do.

I found and continue to find that I have some trust issues that I never really worked through before. In order for me to have a long-lasting relationship and an enduring marriage, my trust needs to be strong. It's an area in which I'm insecure, and I am not afraid to admit my faulty point. I know I am not the only female out there who battles with trust in a relationship. I'm not afraid to admit that even though I am strong in Him, the enemy gets to my head and starts to play scenarios and movie scenes I should never even watch. It's what happens over time when I do not consciously work on my heart and heal from past relationships or my childhood. Not too much ever came through for me when I was younger. Not too many people ever brought hope or did what they said they were going to do without selfish reasons for doing so. I learned to fend for myself and had a very strong attitude about people not helping me with anything. I had an "I can do it myself" attitude.

Bringing past, broken relationships into the mix makes the new relationship even more broken—to an extent. Bringing past soul ties and past strongholds into your current relationship can make things more difficult than you think. You begin to take everything anyone has ever done to you, and you put it on the person you are currently with, which they definitely do not deserve. Every move they make you weigh against something from the past. You may even begin to take something they do and almost make it seem like it is a lie or like they have a hidden agenda to hurt you.

Not everyone is out to "get" you and hurt you.

It is time for you to become a powerful person. I know I was walking around like a powerless victim, always wondering, "Why me? Why did I have such terrible relationships? Why did some of them not want to be with me?" The list can go on. I started losing hope at some points and just thought, "Well, I guess I am supposed to be single. I have to become okay with that." It wasn't the case, though. Deep in my heart I knew I was going to get married. Everything said was always just a pity party I threw myself. It was almost like I wanted people to feel sad for me. I'm typically the type of person who will, when I say something negative, also throw out a positive right after.

When I went through one of the toughest years emotionally it was hard to be positive. I spent most of my time feeling sorry for myself, thinking, "How can this keep happening?" My cousin would always say I am a beautiful and good person, and couldn't understand what I was going through. I think most of the time I put myself into the situation. We always think God brings people into our life, but the enemy does just the same. It is our choice to have the discernment to know what to do. It is our choice to love ourselves enough to let go. It is our job to know our worth.

Your toughest years will seem like your longest years. Just remember that God is continuing to prune you, making you into a better person. In John 15:2 he reminds us:

Every branch in Me that does not bear fruit, He takes away; and every branch that bears fruit, He prunes it so that it may bear more fruit.

I encourage you to open your eyes to a world so much bigger than what you can see right in front of you. We tend to get so lost by what we see that we forget to have faith in what we don't see. When it feels like a tough time, continue to remind yourself of the positive that will come out of it. Think about how you will be able to look back and think, "How did I ever get through that?" You will be able to see the growth and strength that happened inside of you during the time God was pruning you. The thing is, though, we are constantly being pruned. So many people are so unhappy during the whole time of pruning that they waste so many years not enjoying life—not feeling blessed by what is right in front of them. Hours and hours of comparison rob you of your joy for today. So much time is wasted on everyone else's portion instead of seeing the amazing things God has done and given you.

Final Thoughts

IF THERE IS ANYTHING I can leave you with after reading this book, it is to embrace the process and love the journey you are on right now. Everything you are going through has a purpose. One day you will be able to look back on your life and thank God that you got to experience those things. They have made you who you are today and who you will continue to grow to be. It may not make sense right now. You have to just constantly remind yourself that God sees the whole picture. He sees everything. It all makes sense to Him.

And in Your book they were all written, The days fashioned for me.
(Psalm 139:16)

Let's build our faith to be strong so we can believe in all the things that we don't see that God already knows about and has planned for us. If you knew what was coming, you would never doubt. If you knew what was on the other side of what you were going through, you would never complain, cry out to God, need God, or pray, because you would know that it will all be over soon and that it will, in fact, end with a beautiful rainbow. What kind of life would that be—knowing everything that was planned for us? You would never be able to learn and grow. You may not respect things or people. It might be harder to understand how to have a relationship with God. Overall it just wouldn't benefit us as a whole.

Embrace every new season. Enjoy the journey. Be thankful every day for the portion God has given you. Work on making your dreams a reality. Everywhere you go is your ministry and can be a part of your dreams. Don't isolate yourself into one category. Don't isolate God into one category, either. I believe in you and I know you can do this. Don't forget the confidence that you are going to build as you work on loving yourself. The scale doesn't control you. A number doesn't define you. Your body shape doesn't tell people how much you are worth. Tell those close to you that you love them and care about them. Go out and make more memories instead of more projects. There will always be dishes in the sink, laundry to do, and work to be done. Don't miss the moments to love more, care more, understand more, listen more, or help more.

This is your season to know your worth. It's time!

Find Jessica Online:

www.FitCoachJessica.com

www.Instagram.com/JessVaughn22

www.Facebook.com/JessVaughn22

Continue your journey with Jessica at
www.FitCoachJessica.com

46895413R00089

Made in the USA
Lexington, KY
19 November 2015